W9-BFC-111

TERRORIST CHIC

TERRORIST CHIC

An Exploration of Violence in the Seventies

Michael Selzer

HAWTHORN BOOKS, Inc.
Publishers / *New York*
A Howard & Wyndham Company

TERRORIST CHIC: An Exploration of Violence in the Seventies

Copyright © 1979 by Michael Selzer. Copyright
under International and Pan-American Copyright Conventions.
All rights reserved, including the right to reproduce this book
or portions thereof in any form, except for the inclusion of
brief quotations in a review. All inquiries should be addressed
to Hawthorn Books, Inc., 260 Madison Avenue, New York, New York
10016. This book was manufactured in the United States of
America and published simultaneously in Canada by Prentice-Hall
of Canada, Limited, 1870 Birchmount Road, Scarborough, Ontario.

Library of Congress Catalog Card Number: 78–65405

ISBN: 0–8015–7534–6

1 2 3 4 5 6 7 8 9 10

For Miriam and for Sarah

Du hoerest ja,
    von Freud ist nicht die Rede.
Dem Taumel weih ich mich,
    dem schmerzlichsten Genuss,
Verliebtem Hass, erquickendem Verdruss.

——Goethe, *Faust*

I like to feel I'm alive.

——Christopher Makos

Contents

human history. In fact, there is little that is novel in the psychological content or in the forms of Terrorist Chic, which often draws from the precedents of Sade and the Nazis, in particular, to give focus to its perverse imaginings.

Yet in one respect Terrorist Chic is quite novel, for it has succeeded in transforming into a *publicly* acceptable posture what hitherto had existed only in furtive and antisocial privacy. Degenerate fantasies of sex and violence are not new; making them into a fashionable pose *is* something of a departure in the history of culture. It is only in the context of Terrorist Chic that it becomes permissible, even appealing, for *Penthouse* to offer the *bon mot* "Fucking and killing are the same" to its three and a half million readers. Only now, by the same token, might sadomasochistic symbols figure unabashedly in high fashion; or the rewards of stardom be conferred on the singer of a song whose refrain is a joyous "I'm born to kill."

The phenomena here have been labelled *brutality chic* by some. I stick by my term because I believe —a discussion that is taken up more fully in the final chapter—that the kinds of needs that have brought Terrorist Chic into being are the same ones which, on a different level of acting out, have created the fascination with terrorism so widespread in the general population: and in fact have in large measure created terrorism itself.

Terrorist Chic is trashy and not a little trivial. Possibly, it is more repulsive for its triviality than for the fascination with evil and brutality which it flaunts. Yet it is because, rather than despite, these considerations that Terrorist Chic has much to reveal about what is happening to us socially, culturally, and psychologically in the modern world. In a very real sense, Terrorist Chic crystallizes the dilemmas of modernity and suggests some of the possibilities that lie beyond them.

1/ Man's Country

TWO WORLDS MEET AT THE INTERSECTION OF Christopher and West streets on the edge of Manhattan's Greenwich Village. One of these struggles to mask the destructiveness that permeates its reality; the other struggles to assert the reality of the destructiveness it flaunts.

All around, the artifacts of modernity have been abandoned. Huge piers and warehouses line the far side of West, and from there jut out into the Hudson River. Some of these structures collapsed many years ago, or were set ablaze by arsonists. Their barren ruins remain as they were when they fell. Those which still stand, having escaped catastrophe, are merely victims of disaster. Unused, they are considered fair game for amateur urban demolitionists seeking to improve their competence in window-breaking, graffiti-spraying, and similar skills. Rats, packs of wild dogs, and winos unable to find their way back to the Bowery vie with each other for shelter in these caverns.

Along the length of West Street, huge iron pylons support the West Side Highway. Not long ago, the highway was considered the last word in urban planning—an expressway free of traffic lights and intersections that let you speed above the congested streets, from the Battery Tunnel at the tip of Manhattan to the George Washington Bridge north of Harlem, in a matter of minutes.

Bits and pieces of the highway had a tendency to collapse onto the road below, however; and when a truck and an automobile fell through one of these bits (luckily, no one was killed), the city's engineers, having for years failed to maintain the structure properly, closed the whole thing down.

Today it stands—if that's the word—abandoned and sealed off. Visually, its planes continue to violate the lines (horizontal and vertical alike) of the neighborhood. But its incongruity in this respect is now diminished by its lifelessness and by the peeling gray paint on its girders. Dead, it has become more a part of its environment than it ever was when traffic raced over it.

Efforts have been made to salvage something from all this desolation. Two freighters—they look like World War II Liberty ships—have been converted into a floating school. The pier to which they are tied has been cleared and, with some benches near its entrance, is now a favorite sunbathing spot for Villagers by day and a favorite trysting ground for homosexuals by night.

But these pockets of renewal, paltry as they are, will be swept away when, under a project funded by the federal government, all the piers and the West Side Highway are torn down. A new version of the highway —a design whose sterility would have made Le Corbusier ecstatic—will be built at a cost of well over a quarter of a *billion* dollars per mile.

Is this the nemesis of modernity, or its entelechy? The Romans, who were as avid and ambitious builders as we, erected structures, including bridges and aqueducts, which remained viable for centuries. Some, in fact, are still in use today. The Nazis, for their part, not only built neoclassical structures intended to last for a thousand years, but designed them, in accordance with Albert Speer's "theory of ruin value," so that they would look imposing even when they eventually collapsed into ruins.

The necrophilia of Nazi architecture was in service to its grandiosity; it is the other way around for us. We want none of that thousand-year stuff, and our necrophilia demands almost instantaneous gratification. Cut off from the past, it creates a future that is bound to come soon and is bound to be short-lived. Philip Johnson, who only yesterday was perpetrating more forty-story glass boxes than anyone else, has promised us a Chippendale breakfront skyscraper for tomorrow. And the day after?

Build it big so that there will be more to tear down seems to be part of our rule today. Design it inap-

propriately, construct it poorly, maintain it inade-
quately, ignore the reviving effects of a coat of paint or
some flowers, shrug off suggestions that old forms can
be fitted to new functions (which does *not* mean Chippendale): Do all this, and in only a few years you can
apply to the federal government for funds to tear down
the old megastructure and build an even bigger (but no
less ephemeral) one in its place. If Speer wanted buildings to look good when they were in ruins, we want our
buildings to look ruined when they are still good. And
if they don't oblige, ignoring them will make them go
away, or collapse, or burn down. (They are usually so
anonymous anyway that we would hardly notice the
difference.) No Ozymandiases we, our model is the
plutocrat who scraps his Rolls-Royce when it has run
out of gas.

The images on the far side of West Street capture
the simultaneous passions—each requiring the other—
for destruction and renewal which infuse so much of
the modern world.

On the near side of the street, however, fantasies
of destruction search for proof of their own reality.
Such vitality as exists does not stem from these fantasies but merely from the effort to give them reality.

The images proliferate, self-conscious and futile.
"The Impeccable Warrior" is the name of one neighborhood store. Its logo features a muscular Japanese
warrior, a sword held vertically in one hand and his
arms folded in a magnificent posture across his massive chest.

But the store is shut, its window is musty and

anything but impeccable, and the display in it contains only one item, a T-shirt with a map of Manhattan emblazoned on it showing the principal homosexual bars —certainly not the kind of garment in which a warrior of Bushido would look particularly fearful.

Several copies of a poorly printed poster are pasted on a wall nearby. Most of the poster is taken up with a photograph of a man who has tied the mouth of his rifle to the head of another man—an actual news photograph, this—and there is a typewritten caption describing the event in Reuterese. Above the photograph, the word "terminal" is printed in large letters.

What all this means is wholly unapparent to the passing ingenue. Is "terminal" a place where those who get off on this sort of thing (whatever in fact it is) can go and meet their fellows? Is it a play or a movie? Or is it merely the condition one man will be in if the other pulls the trigger? Perhaps it is a political statement. Who knows? A graffito nearby announces, "My heart belongs to me." Another poster announces an "Estrategia Revolucionaria para Liberacion Homosexual," but even if your Spanish were good enough to read beyond the caption, you would have difficulty doing so because someone has defaced the text with the thickly painted words, "Kill Fags!"

The Underground has panache—it is the store sandwiched between the Ramrod and Candyman. An experienced hand has laid out the window displays here, and those displays are quite something. There are pillowcases with "Master" printed on them, and a picture of the master—an eager-looking blond holding a whip in one hand and wearing high black boots and a black leather jacket. He is naked between the top of his boots and the bottom of the waist-length jacket, but that doesn't mean he's forgotten to put on his belt: What we see revealed below it could well serve as the Ramrod's logo, should they decide to acquire one. And if your tastes run in the opposite direction, you can get a "Slave" pillowcase instead.

Five bucks plus tax will bring you a T-shirt with "S/M, B/D, RSVP" printed on it (that's sadomasochism, bondage-domination; the RSVP you already know). And there's far more elaborate equipment, too. Not just the arm-with-clenched-fist dildo ($30, plus tax, where applicable), but penis-handled whips, a wide variety of leather hoods and executioners' masks, discipline collars, spiked wristbands, and maces ("ancient but still effective instrument of punishment"). And for those times when additional restraint is required, how about the Pilgrim Stock, a full-size job imprisoning neck, wrists, and ankles that will only set you back $275?

The salesman inside is young, polite, and, for his métier, quite unobtrusive: His black leather jeans and matching vest, not to mention his spiked wristband and belt, might be considered eccentric in another setting, but fit in perfectly here. The goods displayed in the store, he remarks, are by law "sold as novelties only." The mail-order catalog he gave me (for two dollars) requires customers to sign a statement that "I am purchasing this material exclusively to satisfy my own private interest and curiosity. . . . I will not expose it to any person whose privacy or sensibilities will be offended by the said materials."

One of the *spécialités de la maison* here at the

Underground is an unguent (a very small tube of which
sells for five dollars) called Analeze. Described as a
desensitizing lubricant, it is both cherry flavored and
cherry scented. This concession to convention in a setting as exotic, shall we say, as the Underground comes
as a surprise. Odd, isn't it, that the S/M, B/D crowd is
into *desensitizing* the painful? That the coprophiliacs
want it cherry scented *and* cherry flavored, too? One
would have thought that such sensibilities were strictly
for the Sunday-school crowd.

In fact, not. John Rechy, one of the most know-
ledgeable observers of the deviant-sex scene, reports
(in his *Sexual Outlaw*) that sadomasochistic themes
are proliferating in the sexual underworld. Many
homosexual bathhouses, for instance, now feature at
least one room "constructed to evoke a dungeon, or a
jail cell, replete with chains," he writes. He says too
that a movement called FFA (Fist-Fuckers of America)
is burgeoning.

All the same, it is Rechy's judgment that most of
this kind of thing is "soft core, more fantasy than actuality, involving the charade of pain." He reports that
"ritual whippings, beatings, kickings . . . very rarely
draw real blood." And "Fist-fucking is more talked
about than performed."

Serious injury, even death, has resulted in some
cases, Rechy says, where the actors have been over-
whelmed by the frenzy of their play. But while he believes that fist-fucking, in particular, now occurs with
increasing frequency, it is clear from his account that
the sadomasochistic scene—at least in its homosexual
recension—is *not* one in which the fantasy is acted out

in any concerted and sustained fashion. It is not just a pose or a fad, to be sure, and its roots in the human psyche are obvious enough.

But how depleted that psyche seems to be! Badlands, which straddles the corner of Christopher and West, is a favorite drinking spot for the homosexual black-leather crowd. Its pub sign depicts a wolf baying at the moon, but the picture is so limply executed that it fails utterly to suggest any of the delighted horror for which it is presumably striving.

Inside the bar, too, there is little sense of that horror. The customers are all dauntingly clad in a variety of black leather attire. Keys dangle from studded belts, bandannas flop out of hip pockets on leather jeans, with varying combinations of these signaling different preferences. It is a warm evening, but there are a goodly number of black leather jackets, too. Most of the men without them wear sleeveless undershirts that reveal bulging and often hideously tattooed biceps. Black leather hats, with a chrome chain drawn across the point from where the peak extends, seem *de rigueur.*

It is not an attractive scene, to be sure, and if you try hard you can even feel a little frightened. But what is so startling is the desolation of it all—the lack of vibrancy and excitement at the evocation of what is, after all, one of the most fundamental impulses of our species.

A surge of tension spread through the room when I entered in mufti. But the feeling was not so much one of menace or malevolence toward me as that old minority-group fear of being threatened by strangers.

(Rechy remarks that whereas "straight" homosexuals are increasingly given to assaulting vice-squad cops who raid their hangouts, S & M homosexuals surrender to them with extraordinary timidity: the S's no less than the M's.) Soon my presence was assimilated—not too many cops look like college professors wearing Brooks Brothers suits, after all—and the scene returned to what is evidently normal for it.

Most haunting was the sense of loneliness, which surpassed by far anything you might find in an average singles pickup bar. There was not much noise, except from the scratchy old rock 'n' roll numbers coming out of a jukebox. Occasionally, a small group coalesced and generated a bit of laughter, but that was the exception. Mostly, the people stood as if frozen into postures as lifeless as anything you might see in a store window. In fact, they looked like mannequins. Their postures, as they leaned against the bar or stood coyly in the center of the room, were apparently intended to invite submission—or domination. But they were implausible, even as caricatures. Their empty faces conveyed nothing of the power of their bulging muscles or the sharpness of black leather studded with chrome spikes; their eyes seemed fixed, not in fantasies of prison cells replete with chains but in the effort of evoking such fantasies —and of shielding the self from its isolation and desolation. And contrived as these postures were, they dissolved suddenly when the person moved to another spot in the room or walked out.

So this is what the images of violence come down to in these parts. They are "novelties only," not to be exposed to anyone whose sensibilities they would offend. They are divorced from life—or substitutes for life among these sad, rather than bad, people here. "Genghiz Khan with his wicked weapon looking for new victims. Box 4337" dissolves into the depleted, waxwork figures seen here. A suburban "banquet hall" replete with molded golden furniture and chandeliers made in Hong Kong is more evocative of the splendors of Versailles than this bar is of the terrors of Sade's imaginings.

2/ Son of Arbus

PHOTOGRAPHS, SUSAN SONTAG WRITES (IN *ON Photography*), teach us a new visual code by altering and enlarging our notions of what is worth looking at and what we have a right to observe. They are, she suggests, "a grammar and, even more importantly, an ethics of seeing."

The work of the great American photographers in the first half of this century was influenced by a Whitmanesque vision of populist transcendence. Steichen conferred beauty—and importance—on a milk bottle standing on a tenement fire escape. Hines did the same for a dingy auto-parts store in Atlanta. Like Whitman himself, these photographers did not think that they were abolishing beauty, in Miss Sontag's apt phrase, but that they were generalizing it. The sentimental humanism of Steichen's "Family of Man" exhibition at the Museum of Modern Art (1955) was the ultimate expression of this Whitmanesque erotic embrace of the universe.

This perspective obliterates distinctions of values, the determining role of history, and the imperatives of preference, alike. In their place it offers what is little more than mere schmaltz: "Mankind is one and wonderful." Such a perspective can and usually does become a bore rapidly. And the antidote to life as a bore, Sontag notes, is the aesthete's subversion, which presents life as a horror show instead.

Diane Arbus, whose retrospective exhibition (1972) was the first photographic show to pack in huge crowds at the Museum of Modern Art since "The Family of Man," exemplified this prescription. Where "The Family of Man" universalized the human condition into joy, Sontag points out, Arbus atomized it into horror. Arbus's suicide in 1971, she suggests, "seems to guarantee that her work is sincere, not voyeuristic, that it is compassionate, not cold."

But Sontag judiciously remains unpersuaded. Arbus did not photograph freaks but made freaks of anyone she photographed.

> "You see someone on the street," Arbus wrote, "and essentially what you notice about them is the flaw." The insistent sameness of Arbus' work, however far she ranges from her prototypical subjects, shows that her sensibility, armed with a camera, could insinuate anguish, kinkiness, mental illness, with any subject. Two

photographs are of crying babies; the babies look disturbed, crazy . . .

"Paper-ghosts and a sharp-eyed witty program of despair," Sontag concludes, are all that is left over of Whitman's discredited dream of cultural revolution.

It is a legacy of effortless and undiscriminating hostility. It not only invites the photographer to be a combatant, but requires that he be one. The enemy is society, humanity. And the objectives of the campaign? They remain obscure, and probably are not and never were particularly important: *"Qu'importe les victimes si le geste est beau?"*

"A shock, these images!" the French magazine *Photo* reported breathlessly, seeing in them further evidence of "the fabulous golden age" of New York photography and of Arthur Tress's position as a leader of its avant-garde.

And shocking these images are: A naked man lies spread-eagled on a railroad track littered with debris; a huge tank car looms up behind him. Or a naked man, his face in a leather mask, sits against the wall of a squalid, decaying room; electric wires lead from his body to a large clock. Or, again: In a room even more decaying than the previous one, a naked man kneels with his head in a bucket. An empty boot is on his back. You are probably getting the picture by now, but if not, here's another. A man squats on the floor, an upturned funnel on his head like a dunce's cap. A woman stands over him holding a chain and mace that dangle in front of his face. A bucket shields her head, her arms conceal her breasts, and dark shadows obscure her pudenda so that it is only with difficulty that you establish her sex.

Un choc, ces images! And there are many more.

It was not always so. A Brooklyn boy, Arthur Tress graduated from Bard College in 1962 and then headed west. He moved around Mexico and California, where he studied Spanish and painting, and photographed Indian tribes and deserted lumber towns.

Next, he traveled to Japan, where he lived in a Buddhist monastery and studied flower arrangement. From there he went to Thailand, where he also lived in a Buddhist monastery; and then to India, where he photographed the fishing villagers of Kerala and the tribesmen of the Nilgiri mountains. After India, he lived in Stockholm for two years, and then, in 1968, he returned to the United States. Back in New York he did a series of photographs of a Kabuki production, and then went to work for VISTA, photographing black sharecroppers in South Carolina, Chinese immigrants in California, and so on. A Sierra Club exhibition in New York, "Open Spaces in the Inner City" (1971), was the first exhibition of his photographs to attract major critical attention.

Up to this point, the sensibilities and subjects of Tress's work—and, indeed, the pattern of his wanderings—were those of many a gifted and susceptible child of the sixties. But Arthur had had a very unhappy childhood; he carried a portrait of Kafka in his camera bag, and his work now began to express and explore the unresolved turmoil of his soul.

His first book, *The Dream Collector* (1972), was a

series of haunting tableaux of dreams re-enacted for the camera. It is a powerfully plausible work, profoundly disturbing in its eerie and persistent evocations of the unconscious. Nevertheless, Tress managed to fit a few wish-fulfilling dreams into this tapestry of psychic deprivation. Tress's next book, *Shadow* (1975), a sort of autobiographical novel in photographs, actually concludes with a promise of redemption: "And he left his cave glowing and strong as a morning sun that comes out of the dark mountains." In 1977, the series of brutal sadomasochistic images entitled "Phallic Fantasies," some of which we described earlier, was shown at the Alfred Stieglitz Gallery in Manhattan.

And so the question arises: How does a nice boy from Brooklyn—one who has studied flower arrangement in a Buddhist temple in Japan and worked for VISTA—come to be taking this kind of photograph nowadays? Sure, no one expects Arthur to spend his life arranging flowers, and I don't even know whether VISTA exists any longer. The artist grows, evolves, moves into new areas of inquiry. That's all very fine and how things should be. But *this?*

"Fist-fucking is like giving birth," Arthur the epigrammatist now declares publicly. "What is the meaning hidden in the sadomasochistic passions which explode in our thoughts?" he asks. "Are they really abnormal, or are they trying to show us something we refuse to see? I think that the function of photography is to reveal what is secret, even if it remains obscure for the majority of people."

So much for the public posture: Arthur the shocker, Arthur the teacher. The photographer as

Freud. "What's very interesting in my work," he told me when I visited him in his cramped studio apartment on Manhattan's Upper West Side, "is that I just let it flow out, you know. I've liberated myself as an artist. . . . I think that's what's interesting about my work. There's a great deal of honesty in it."

These protestations surfaced periodically in our conversation. He is not, Arthur says, a phenomenon of the times—unlike certain other photographers whom he can and does mention by name. "An artist tries to psych out the times," he explains. "I feel I have transcended what society throws at me, and use it for my art."

There is nothing ephemeral about his current work's preoccupation with violence, he went on to say. "It exists in everyone, these deep, disturbing areas of violence, torture, hostility, anger, destruction. They're not necessarily negative but exist in a very therapeutic way inside the human mind. It's like Greek tragedy: Most art deals with the very basic. All mythic material has this violence in it."

He hastened to add, however, that he never does anything violent himself. "I'm very into Japanese art. I'm very calm. When people come to pose for me, we have fun, the models have fun, it's like a game. I'm portraying violence, but it's a bit of an acting-out of things people don't really do."

Indeed, it turned out that not only is sadomasochism "not done all that seriously," but that it has "little relationship to the needs people really have." The sadomasochistic posing so fashionable today, Tress argues, "is merely one of a series of outfits that people put on. It's not their real voice. It's just decor. It has no metaphysical position in it. Six months from now, these same people will be doing whatever's new and trendy then." Sadomasochistic imagery in most people's work is contrived, he added; the pose "just happens to be in vogue right now." And he expressed his "war-weariness of all these constant styles, new things, that are coming along all the time."

I was becoming confused. Arthur, it seemed, is into violence even though he's not, really, since it is merely a passing fad of the time that no one takes seriously. Yet he happens to be photographing it, even though, as an artist, he transcends his time and there is a great deal of honesty in his work. To resolve all this perplexity, I therefore asked him whether he would be doing work like "Phallic Fantasies" if sadomasochism was *not* in vogue. His answer was unequivocal.

"No. I would like to say I would, but I'm very much someone who does what people want," he answered. He was very broke last August, he explained, and met a Cuban publisher of pornographic homosexual magazines who asked him to work for him at a hundred dollars a page, and that is how he got into this series of photographs.

Why, I asked him next, does he *not* act out the sadomasochistic fantasies expressed in his newest work. Again the answer was unequivocal. "They're not my fantasies," Tress replied. "I interview people and get their fantasies and photograph them."

"But how can you make art out of other people's fantasies?" I asked. "Isn't that contrived?"

"What's wrong with contrivance?" he countered.

"It isn't authentic," I said. "Beauty is truth, re-member, and art is honest."

"It's a very narrow tightrope I'm walking be-tween the authentic and the contrived. Occasionally, what I've contrived becomes very authentic."

"Or is it that photography makes it *seem* authen-tic?" I asked.

But Tress was more interested in talking about the sadomasochistic experience than about its authen-ticity. "I don't think sadomasochism is nihilistic," he said. "It's just another way of people communicating with each other. If I photograph Riverside Park, it's not that I'm telling everyone to come and sit there. And in the same way, my photographs do not assert a violent life-style."

"But you're not communicating anything of yourself in your photographs, are you?" I persisted. "And you're not just stating a fact of human nature. You're inviting people to revel in it."

"I love it. It's very interesting. I love to revel. What's wrong with that?"

"But you *don't* revel in it! That's just the point! How can you revel in a contrived fantasy which you've taken from other people from whom, as you say, it's not even real in the first place and is no more than just one garment in a large wardrobe? And how can you claim to love it if that's so?"

"That's my way of getting round to the truth. They're not fantasies, really, my photographs. They're more like folk art."

"But folk art isn't commissioned and it doesn't

remain in vogue for six months before giving way to something else," I replied.

"All this is striking certain mythic patterns, you see," Tress explained. "And that's why it's authentic."

"No one is challenging that violence is rooted in human nature—perhaps for good as well as for bad. But what I'm trying to get at is the *genuineness* of your experience of it. You said earlier that you're a very calm person. Later, you added that your ideal is to have a nice house in East Hampton and a lover who has plenty of money, and that you wouldn't want to photograph all that because it would be so dull! Doesn't love —and for that matter, luxury, too—strike certain mythic patterns?"

"Yes, of course," he replied. "And in my work now I'm only doing images of tenderness . . ."

"Oh!"

3/Haute Couture: Going Out in Style

A THREE-QUARTER-LENGTH EVENING DRESS of delicately tinctured purple. Full, yet light and diaphanous, so that its folds fall in thin, graceful rivulets rather as they might on a Greek statue. A petticoat reaches up only to the waist, leaving the flawless breasts of the model clearly visible under the transparent cloth. A beautiful dress. A beautiful woman. Both exquisitely feminine and more than slightly risqué. A charming, dream-inspiring image—

—except when photographed by Helmut Newton, one of the world's leading fashion photographers. In Newton's photograph, the setting is a motel in Key Biscayne at night, and the model is running across the lawn with a look of stark terror on her face. The "news photograph" tone is heightened by the shadow of the model cast by a flashgun. What is the girl running away from? We don't know. But a possible source of her wide-eyed fear may be discovered in the slash of red across her throat. Is it a necklace? It seems unlikely, for it is about three inches high and does not fit the dress. In any case, it is difficult to tell. Artfully, the red is some-what blurred. It could be an inappropriate necklace. It could be raw flesh.

Equally renowned as a fashion photographer is Mr. Newton's compatriot, Chris von Wangenheim. Among Wangenheim's images is a series of advertise-ments for Dior. In one, there is a beautiful model wear-ing a beautiful fur coat; the automobile she's standing next to has been set on fire. Its vicious flames light up the night sky.

Another Wangenheim masterpiece: a gorgeous bracelet by Dior, a gorgeous woman, whose gorgeous wrist is being chewed by a Doberman pinscher. To ad-vertise Dior sunglasses, Wangenheim shows a white Venetian blind, a few slats of which are pulled up by an incredibly sinister-looking woman in shades. You know she's not checking to see what the weather is. Is she a hit person making sure the job's been done?

These two Germans, it should be said, are also much in demand outside the realm of fashion photog-raphy. One of Newton's famous shots is of the face of a beautiful woman, her eyelids heavily shadowed with gold dust. Or at least one of the eyelids is. You can't tell about the other because she's holding a piece of raw meat to it.

"My father," Newton comments, "used to say, 'My boy, you'll end up in the gutter!' "

When I visited Wangenheim in his New York

studio, he showed me one of his most recent works, the sleeve of an album put out by a German rock group called Dracula. The picture is one of those two-kicks-for-one deals. You see the beautiful naked back of one lady who is being hugged by another beautiful lady: That's one kick. An abundance of blood flows from the neck of the first: That's the other kick. Wangenheim, by the way, says that he is no longer into this kind of thing. He does not want to talk about it. He does not want to talk about why he is no longer into it. He has become —very reticent.

But these macabre, menacing photographs are not the exclusive preserve of Germans. There is a remarkable series done by Gianpaolo Barbieri for Versace advertisements. In one, a very beautiful and very dead woman lies in a clear Perspex cylinder; another, alive but staring in fright off to one corner, stands behind her. In the next shot, three beautiful women are staring at a fourth. She too is dead. One of the women has an expression of curiosity as she gazes at her dead companion. A second looks on with manifest pleasure. A third expresses only indifference. In the final photograph, all four are alive and seemingly well. Their faces have been made up to look very severe, however. Three have their hair pulled tightly to the back of their heads, the fourth has an electrifying Afro, and all are gazing transfixedly at some kind of weird electrical apparatus. In all three photographs, by the way, the women are wearing charmingly simple, even naïve, dresses.

Another Versace advertisement is infused with a quite different kind of malevolent mystery. We see the legs of a figure in semimilitary uniform running across a marble floor. Sprawled on the floor is a beautiful woman in a beautiful dress. She is holding on desperately to one of the uniformed legs. What is happening? There is no way of knowing for sure. But that something dangerous and violent is taking place is immediately apparent.

Many fashion-magazine layouts reflect the same mood as these advertisements. A four-page feature in *Mode International* is devoted to photographs of two beautiful women wearing trench coats. The ladies are incredibly sinister-looking and conjure up memories of Bogart in his more malevolent roles. They are in an otherwise deserted and almost totally dark restaurant, scowling viciously in a couple of photographs, poring over newspapers spread on a table in another. Later, either because other things have been afoot all the time, or else to console each other for some failure (the bomb didn't explode?) or to celebrate some success (the bomb *did* explode!), we find them in poses more becoming the Daughters of Bilitis than the daughters of Bogey.

Here are more glimpses to titillate one's fancy. *Vogue* wants to show its readers what the well-dressed woman of the bicentennial year is wearing. One tends to forget that in view of the action, however. It is night, and a woman is about to step into a glorious antique limousine, but her movement is arrested as she catches sight of another woman who's been trailing her and who is pointing her hand at her. But it's a dark night, it's a dark limousine, and the cloak that the second woman is wearing obscures just what it is that she is pointing at the other. Could it be a pistol?

Another *Vogue* feature—this time on perfumes— shows an elegantly gowned woman staring motionless across a darkly lit street. We see her from the rear and are impressed by how charmingly her wrists cross one another as they are held in place by handcuffs. "Is she a prisoner of love?" the caption asks. We can only hope so . . .

. . . But perhaps she is "The Killer" captioned in another *Vogue* feature, this one of the season's new shoes, fitted on dainty feet that are energetically destroying some electronic equipment. It seems a bit far-fetched to call a mere machine-smasher a killer, but for all we know, that could be life-support equipment she is demolishing—and probably is.

For the closest thing to the real thing, however, you have to leave the two dimensions of the glossy page and turn to those treasure caves that line the canyons of Manhattan—the display windows of the fashionable stores. Here's one: At Bendel's, on Fifty-seventh Street, seven ladies stand jauntily in a straight line in the window. They look great but can see nothing, since their eyes are masked with bandagelike blindfolds. One of them has an apple on her head, and we can only hope that the firing squad is going to aim at that.

Also at Bendel's: Five women dressed in wonderful autumnal colors are bound together by more than just the seasonal motif. The thick strands of rope by which they are tied are held—at the far end of the window—by a mean-looking cowboy. His skill with the lasso is, evidently, greatly appreciated by the lady standing just behind him. It is obvious that she will join in whatever tricks he is planning for his captives once he has dragged them back to the corral.

Another Bendel's window shows three women in evening clothes—one a tie-dyed number that looks as if it were splattered with blood—standing, as if cowering, in the corner of a room. At their feet another woman is sprawled on the floor. She seems very dead, and whatever was in the bottle in her hand has turned her body green.

Heading east, you pass by Bonwit Teller. Here a window is crisscrossed with black masking tape to make it look like a prison cell. A black sphere floats at the rear and to one side of the window. In front of it stands a woman in a very white suit and very black and big sunglasses. The whole setting could be from a James Bond movie filmed in black-and-white. Another Bonwit window has a lovely young woman in a lovely evening dress standing rather forlornly in a room from whose ceiling dangle several ropes. Perhaps she is contemplating suicide. But the ropes are cut at different lengths, so it seems more probable that she is the last of a gang that has presented a morning's arduous work for the hangman.

Over at Bloomingdale's there is a huge wooden model (the kind they use in art classes, with all those joints) bound in belts just the way some of the patrons down at the Underground might fancy. Things have gone a bit far here, however. The model has its neck twisted at a dangerous angle—nay, a fatal one, a circumstance explainable in terms of the belt suspended from the ceiling, within which the neck is caught.

Up a few blocks, at Halston's, we find five glossy metallic mannequins attired in incongruously wispy and delicate evening gowns. The room is bare of furniture, but a portable TV set and record player sit on the floor. Someone has smashed them and a large number of champagne bottles that are also scattered around the floor. Brutal intruders, perhaps? Or just the girls having fun in their own special way?

These displays are striking, no doubt about it. Along with the new wave of advertisements and fashion-magazine layouts, they have introduced a fresh excitement—in fact, sensationalism—to haute couture. And according to *The Wall Street Journal,* they have also boosted sales.

What Gene Moore, a prominent display director, has to say about windows holds true of the other media, too: "Windows should give an emotional reaction of either pleasure—or yuk! You know, there has to be an emotional reaction or else you're a failure."

Pleasure or yuk. Or, perhaps, pleasure *and* yuk: the pleasure of yuk. What is noteworthy, though, is the arbitrariness of this yukky pleasure and its basic purposelessness. You remember the images but not the objects to which they are attached. The ominous, sinister, violent *timbre* remains in the mind long after you have forgotten what "the killer" shoes looked like or what clothes the ladies who are about to be shot by the firing squad at Bendel's were wearing. You not only forget these quickly, you scarcely note them at the time.

The settings are violent in their intent, but they are also violent in their disregard for the garments they are ostensibly displaying.

The recognized pioneer of the new wave of window displays is twenty-nine-year-old Robert Currie, until recently director of visual planning at Bendel's. Like several other people whom we will be meeting in this book, Currie was a sixties activist, dedicatedly opposing the war in South Vietnam and working with blacks in the South as a VISTA volunteer. He spent two years in a Catholic seminary studying for the priesthood, but gave that up in favor of his present career.

In his earliest work, Currie moved dramatically away from the traditional stylized poses of window displays and created tableaux in which clothes were shown in everyday settings—women waiting on line to get into a movie, women in a laundromat, and so on. Not exactly the kind of situation you would expect to be familiar to the women who shop at Bendel's, perhaps, but the realism of the windows caused a sensation. Encouraged, Currie moved into more risqué areas. One window that was a great success showed his women in a subway station with "Fuck You!" graffitoed on the walls. But there was more to come.

In the sixties, Currie says, he had felt very idealistic and self-sacrificing—hence VISTA and his try for the priesthood. The seventies, for him, brought freedom from what the sixties had been all about. "Earlier," he explained, "I wouldn't allow myself to be aware of myself. My growing up changed that. I now allow myself things I wouldn't have ten years ago."

He spoke with a naughty grin. "We're living in an

age of depravity," he went on. "If you're not aware that depravity exists in New York City, certainly, then you're not aware."

"In what way does depravity exist in New York?" I asked him.

"Well, just compare the squalor of Fourteenth Street—the junkies, the winos, the bag-ladies—compare that to the comfort of my apartment!"

"It's a big contrast," I agreed. "But it sounds very much like sixties talk to say that the fact of that contrast means we're depraved. In any case, surely that contrast is not what your windows are all about?"

"Of course, you're right!" Currie answered laughingly. "But my windows *are* making a social comment." I asked what the nature of the comment was— and about what section of society it was being made.

"Depravity may not be overt," he said. "But certainly from where I go and from what my friends tell me, I can see depravity in styles of life. *My* life style is depraved. I go to the sleaziest bars in town. My sexual conduct is depraved. And since we're in an age of depravity, I thought there should be a comment on it, and I'm commenting on it in my windows. I think I'm a product of my time. Ten years ago I wasn't aware of depravity. Now I am."

"But surely you can't say society is depraved just because you and your friends are?" I objected. "Unless, of course, you have very, very many more friends than most people have! I don't see in what way your depraved windows are mirroring a social phenomenon. Do they reflect your own preferences merely, or are they really making a social comment?"

"They're a part of society today, aren't they?"

"Are you saying that your evidence for the fact that these are depraved times is the depraved windows you lay out?"

Currie laughed good-naturedly. "Look, it's like this. I play to the sophisticated, aesthetic audience of people who shop at Bendel's. I think they are all aware of depravity, but I guess my windows make them even more aware of it. I guess I feel a need to make people see that depravity exists, and then everybody becomes more aware of it. I guess I was just trying to make it more concrete.

"And what's more," he continued, "lots of people are making the same kind of comment nowadays, and if they are, depravity is part of what is happening and that is why they're making these comments."

"But how persuasive is that, really?" I asked. "Don't all these people know each other, or at least know of each other's work?"

"I guess so, sure. We're probably talking about thirty people, no more."

"So if all of these people were to disappear from the scene, then possibly there would be no one around making comments about today's depravity?"

"Yeah, I guess so. Perhaps we're not mirroring reality but making it more real. You see, it's all very real for us, and what we're doing is making it part of the social scene. We're making a social phenomenon, you could say."

He found this recognition amusing and laughed with that good-humored chuckle which had punctuated much of our conversation. He went on to say that

He acknowledged that the "depravity" in his displays is something of a contrivance. It creates the semblance of a social reality that is made to seem all the more substantial by the three-dimensionality of the medium in which he works, but it is, as a social phenomenon, quite artificial. "Psychologically, though," he hastened to add, "it's real enough."

"Since you're a master craftsman of social pseudo-reality," I asked him, "can you tell me what's going to come next?"

"I'm a visionary and see ahead of my times," he replied in a matter-of-fact way. "I would never do a depraved window again. It's no longer valid. How long can people continue to see depravity on Fifty-seventh Street or Lexington Avenue without getting bored to death? One gets bored with everything, we get very jaded. I'm not really totally jaded yet"—he paused to chuckle again—"but I feel different about my windows. I'm making a new kind of comment now."

"And that is?"

"I'm into purity of form now. Beauty: That's where my head is at."

"And whatever happened to the depravity?"

"There's still a direct connection between me and my work," he insisted. "Physically, and to some extent mentally, I'm into depravity; but my work, my aesthetics, is into beauty. Anyway, there's beauty in depravity. Just look at Helmut Newton's work and tell me if that isn't so. Perhaps I'm also synthesizing beauty and depravity right now. But my work is definitely leading away from depravity to beauty."

"Do you think there's something flighty, superfi-

trying to make people not fear their environment—to soften the blow, if you will. And exposing violence is not as shocking today as it would have been ten years ago. In fashion it's startling; it attracts you to the picture so that you remember it. There's a freedom in design that just wasn't there even five years ago. It's very exciting now. We can explore methods which have never been explored before. Creative people are constantly striving for some new concept. It's healthy to get into different things, otherwise you get bored so quickly."

He spoke in a thoughtful manner even as his remarks meandered from point to point. The current obsession with violence has a novel dimension, he remarked, which is also reflected in fashion. In particular, terrorism appeals to the imagination. It is fascinating. And it has taught people that there's an end in sight for the world . . .

"Yes, an end in sight for the world is what I said," Birch confirmed. "The violence in the world is going to go on and on until we all blow ourselves up or destroy the world. But the space program has shown us that there's another place, and so when everything ends here, we'll be able to go there—to some other planet or whatever—and start off anew. So we know there's a way out, and if that's the case, then violence is nothing to get all *that* upset about."

Birch was adamant, however, that his work does not convey any messages of violence or, indeed, messages of any kind whatsoever. He is against the "narrative" trend in window display, which, he explained, detracts from the merchandise it is supposed to be promoting. The preoccupation with violence and terrorism is very much in vogue just now, he said, but it does not make any business sense at all, since women simply are not going to wear the kinds of *outré* clothing that some of the French and Italian designers are trying to slip them into. This is not, Birch insists, a political or moral judgment, only a practical one. "It doesn't matter what we do," he added, referring to the end of the world. "It's going to happen anyway."

Birch has very definite standards about what is and what is not proper. "Putting a cigarette into a mannequin's hand is vulgar," he told me. "I think that is something you shouldn't throw at the public."

Beyond such considerations, however, his work is dictated only by the demands of design, texture, color, and space. "I'm not trying to characterize anything in my displays," he said when I asked him about the lady who is about to be hanged and also about that very James Bond–like window. "Certainly I'm not trying to depict violence. Violence is everywhere—just open the newspapers and you'll see that—but I am not a violent person. Violence scares me. My windows don't evoke *anything* to me. My concern is only for design, and I use the space and the objects just as designs. I don't intend any emotional impact at all. I feel a purely *visual* excitement when I look at my windows and think of how they happened, how I put them together —but they don't evoke anything other than that for me."

On reflection, he added, "All the violence every-

where . . . It's probably affecting me unconsciously. But
I don't feel it."

    I had a little chat about these matters with Alex-
ander Liberman, the dapper, elderly expatriate Eng-
lishman who is the editorial boss of *Vogue.* Mr. Liberman speaks with the kind of hauteur you might think
existed only on the faces of *Vogue* models, and for
much of our conversation took the position that I was
seeing a trend where none existed, that I was making
a mountain out of a molehill, that there were no images
of cruelty and violence in contemporary fashion and,
least of all, in *Vogue* itself. Referring to "The Killer"
caption of the feature about shoes, he actually suggested that it was *I* who was applying a violent conno-
tation to the layout.

    Vogue, Liberman explained, comes out twelve
times a year and has some hundred pages of editorial content per issue. The range of subjects covered
in the magazine, on the other hand, is rather limited
—clothes, shoes, scarves, perfumes, and the like. And
so there is the problem of finding new ways of presenting these recurring items. Boredom must be avoided at almost any cost. How do you go on and on
making that bottle of perfume look exciting? One
way is to do something like the "prisoner of love"
photograph, which creates an entirely new context
for the presentation.

    I pointed out that this must be a problem that
Vogue has faced for several decades, but that it is only
in the past few years that it has attempted to deal with
it by these suggestions of violence. Why, I asked Liber-

man, have these particular motifs come along just now?

He replied that the past few years have witnessed the liberation of creative imagination, and that photographers such as Chris von Wangenheim and Helmut Newton had not been around earlier. He then went on to point the finger at the media, and at literature and our times in general. "We're swamped with visions of violence," he said, "and I think that in all modern literature, newspapers, and so on, violence stimulates. We are in an era that is attracted to violence. Murders are played up in the newspapers—it's the biggest headline. Death has a fascination, and people will buy that kind of headline."

Liberman was adamant, though, that *Vogue* would never lend itself to "any form of human degradation if it's taken on a serious level. Things that are truly morally wrong, such as sadism: We wouldn't do them, we wouldn't even consider them."

The killer shoes and the prisoner of love and the woman who is being mugged or kidnapped or whatever else is happening to her in the bicentennial issue do not, in Liberman's view, represent sadism or cruelty or violence or anything like that "on a serious level." They are, rather, merely "entertainment." They give "a little seasoning, pepper, surprise, to the printed page," he claimed. "When we do a picture of a dog biting a leg," he went on to say, "we don't think that's a cruel picture, we think it is an amusing and provocative situation. What is more, these pictures widen the tolerance of readers. It's good to expose them to things that are beyond the accepted norms."

A very gracious and competent and mirthful lady is Mary Lee Fletcher, who heads the Christian Dior operation in the United States. I wanted to know about the startling Wangenheim ads that Dior has been running for the past few months, and Miss Fletcher invited me to have lunch with her and an associate in the very genteel offices Dior maintains in New York so that we could talk about them.

"Everyone is telling me that there's a lot of social significance behind the campaign we are running," Miss Fletcher said as we cut into our steaks. "That's nonsense! I know how it started: It was a completely advertising thing. The Doberman pinscher came up because we were discussing how we were going to highlight the jewelry, what we could do, and I think Chris had just seen or done something with that marvelous dog"—this may have been the picture of the dog biting the woman's leg which Wangenheim did for *Vogue.* "It was the most terrific dog I've ever seen, by the way. Between takes, he would go up on my lap, that's how fierce he was!

"Anyway," Miss Fletcher continued, "Chris suggested this, and we thought that maybe that would be a terrific idea. We could have drama, we could have a magnificent-looking blond there with the darkness of the dog as a play-off. It would be very exciting visually, and then we could draw the eye down to the jewelry. And that's how it all came about. We were not making social comments but trying to come up with a good advertisement. And we're very happy with the results. We couldn't have done a more successful campaign— people are still talking about it."

"Why was it necessary to choose a Doberman? That's so obviously an attack dog," I pointed out.

"Maybe I'm being too simplistic about it all," Miss Fletcher replied. "But I don't see anything violent in that dog. He's not biting her. He's just gently holding her wrist. Dog lovers love that ad!" She laughed and then said, "I think everyone's taking this much too seriously!"

"What about the lady with that car on fire?" I asked. "Are you telling me that it only got overheated?"

"The girl is just walking by on the street. She's not related to the car."

"She just *happens* to be walking past a car that's on fire?" I asked skeptically.

"Yes," Miss Fletcher replied with an abundance of good cheer. "This sort of thing happens on the street occasionally. By the way, the man who set it up for us was the person who did the special effects for *The Godfather*.

"You see," she continued, "we needed drama. A little poodle sitting on the lap playing with the wrist is not going to get me people looking at the ad and talking about it. You don't want an ad that looks like something that's come out of a mail-order catalog."

I pressed her. Women in expensive fur coats don't just happen to pass cars on fire. And the Doberman *did* have his teeth around the woman's wrist—one tooth was actually at the point of puncturing her skin.

The tone of the advertisements seemed inescapably sinister and violent.

By way of reply, Miss Fletcher quoted the results of a recent survey Dior had commissioned to find out what shoppers in expensive department stores felt about these ads. It seems that a large majority of women reacted favorably to them and that they did not respond to the suggestions of violence in them. Instead, they remarked that the photographs were striking, beautiful, appealing, sexy, and so on. Only a small proportion of the women interviewed appear to have noticed the violence, and almost all of these thought that the ads were, as a result, in poor taste.

"You see," Miss Fletcher said triumphantly, "it all depends on what you read into them. You know, ABC wanted to interview me about them because they thought the ads were sensuous, and CBS wanted to interview me about them because they thought the ads were brutal!"

There was much laughter over this, and I suggested that perhaps someone at NBC was reading his Freud and would soon want to interview Miss Fletcher because he recognized that these ads were both brutal *and* sensuous.

It is astonishing that, apparently, most people do not consider these ads violent: not just well-heeled women in fashionable stores but—again, apparently— people who are as involved in the fashion business as the heads of *Vogue* and Dior. Freud has something to say about this, too, in *The Introductory Lectures on Psychoanalysis.*

An artist, he suggests, understands how to elaborate his daydreams so that they lose that personal note which grates on other people and thus become enjoyable to others. Also, he knows how to modify them so that their origin in prohibited psychological sources *is not easily detected,* and how to "attach to this reflection of his fantasy life so strong a stream of pleasure that, for a time at least, the repressions are outbalanced and dispelled by it."

All this implies either that Mr. Liberman and Miss Fletcher are far less perceptive, or that Messrs. Currie, Birch, and Wangenheim are far greater artists than one might have suspected.

Fashion's current preoccupation with violence, however, seldom becomes explicit in the actual merchandise, and is basically irrelevant to it.

True: If you seek you will find. There's a grim, black, get-thee-behind-me ski suit called "Satan," which Anba markets for $250. Following the idea through, you can top off this outfit with Shoei's black racing helmet, a space-age affair with a huge reflecting visor that masks the face with shiny sleekness guaranteed to protect your anonymity.

If you are not athletically inclined—or if you are, perhaps for *après-ski*—Claude Montana will be happy to slip you into a multi-zippered leather suit. Its massively padded shoulders and matching high-peaked cap are just the kind of thing Julius Streicher might have doodled while daydreaming about the centennial edition of *Der Stürmer.*

But the Paris houses are rather limited, and for

a wider selection of this sort of froufrou you have to go over to Italy. There, Silvano Malta and Enrico Coveri are among the leading exponents of what the Italian *Vogue* calls the *"fascino del nero maledetto."* Ah, that wicked, wicked black! With a measure of historical myopia, *Vogue* would have us believe that Enrico and Silvano and their friends *"infrange tutte le norme"* with their designs. But let's not get into *"nero"* as a motif in recent Italian sartorial history: We'll assume Il Duce's wife dressed him in those black shirts so she wouldn't have to worry about ring around the collar of *her* man . . .

The fashion reporters cause much excitement with news of "neo-Nazi" and "terrorist" statements being made in recent designs from Paris and Rome, but the fact is that very little of this kind of apparel goes out into the market or even appears in the fashion magazines. Very little of it, in fact, even gets designed. The hype is pervasive, but to all intents and purposes it is confined to the promotional side of fashion and leaves virtually no imprint on the clothes and accessories that are sold and worn. At this writing, for example, Yves Saint Laurent promises a day "bomb" and an evening "bomb" in his fall fashions, thereby reflecting (as Mary Russell breathlessly tells readers of *The New York Times* [April 2, 1978]) "the heavy influence of politics." But the betting is that these "bombs" are going to be fairly tame, and that women wearing them will look a lot more like sexy bombshells than like walking, talking thermonuclear devices.

Politics, of course, does not presuppose bombs,

and this kind of silly sensationalism could be dismissed contemptuously were it not for the fact that it has become such an important part of the mystique that surrounds high fashion and lends it a distinctive excitement.

Where implicitly brutal, sadomasochistic motifs are widely found—sold, that is, and actually worn by people, as opposed to merely being hyped by advertisers and PR men—they do not come to us from Paris or Rome but straight from our forefathers, the flower children. Many a hippie craftsperson, you may remember, worked in leather, and belts were among their most widely manufactured products. Not since Byron swathed his waist with rainbow-hued sashes to hide his corpulence has this modest but potentially pernicious (watch out, you, if you're planning to *infrange tutte le norme!*) item received so much attention. Big, thick belts were particularly à la mode, of course; and from these attention turned to belt buckles. New versions of these proliferated so rapidly that soon one hesitated to turn up at a peace rally without one's own, customized clasp.

In the early seventies Frye showed the way from sandals to boots, and suddenly everyone was into boots, too. Many of these still evoke the rustic fantasies of the sixties, but please note that the boundary between them and the pseudomacho, pseudosadomasochistic fantasies of today is becoming increasingly vague (almost imperceptibly, the homesteader becomes the cowboy). And, of course, boots *have* developed into more explicitly fearsome objects, particularly for women (most recently, as accessories to the neo-military look that is coming in).

Women, in general, have kept a step or two ahead of the minority sex with regard to belts, too. They were the first to get into bandolier-type belts, and then into cartridge-case belts, and from there it was only natural that chains should start to proliferate on their dainty waists, soon to twine their way around slender necks and wrists as well.

But a lot of this is well sublimated—do those little 14-karat links *really* suggest bondage? More to the point, however, these somewhat remote evocations of violence and terror, these suggestions of kinky fetish regalia, are about as far as most people seem willing to go in the clothes they actually wear. The fantastic sick-chic creations of some of the French and Italian salons are nowhere to be seen in real life; the advertising hype may encourage fantasy, but it has failed to become reified. It is one thing to step down Fifth Avenue or to walk through your suburban shopping mall wearing less than totally discreet belts and boots—but we are just not ready yet to parade around looking like the son or daughter of Mussolini.

Leather jackets, on the other hand, are quite current—even black motorcycle, Hell's Angels, storm-trooper numbers with heavy chromed zippers. But these are basically replacements for the old army combat jackets that were so fashionable among the flower children of the sixties and that have now, alas, worn out. And even though the punks love them, their mean message has fairly well been covered up by the fact that they are now so commonplace. This does not mean the message isn't there, however.

A great fashion among the young people in Western Europe is the so-called Yasir Arafat scarf, which the kids wrap around their heads or necks or waists, or use to mask their faces whenever they turn up for the funeral of a Bader-Meinhof gang member or a similar event. But the Yasir Arafat scarf is actually just the Bedouin *kaffiyeh,* or headdress, and actually it is at least as much King Hussein as it is Yasir Arafat, although if the kids like to think of themselves in terms of the latter there's nothing much anyone can do about it.

A much more substantial revolution in fashion has, in fact, gone in the very opposite direction of Terrorist Chic. Femininity is now flaunted to the point where the female body is virtually denuded—at least from the waist up. There's nothing terrible about this unless you are a born-again Christian or Hassid, but there is no denying that it is a major revolution in the way women dress. Not since the heyday of Napoleon have they revealed so much of their unfettered breasts and let their nipples protrude—or otherwise—at will.

This development too has its origins in the sixties. With the advent of women's liberation, many women stopped wearing their bras, not realizing, perhaps, how greatly men would appreciate this particular form of protest; and the sexual permissiveness which was also a part of the sixties furthered this trend. The point, though, is that this is a real trend in fashion—something one can observe in any office building or on any street in America today, and which will continue to be around five years from now. It has a factuality that the pseudotrend represented by the Wangenheims, the Curries, the Montanas, and others simply does not possess. Perhaps it signifies that a woman today would sooner see herself as a sex object than as a crypto-terrorist or neo-Nazi. But surely it is gratifying to know that the sexy, succoring breast has triumphed where the *fascino del nero maledetto* has failed.

4 / Dracula

REGINE, THE DISCOTHEQUE QUEEN, KNOWS
where it's at and lays it on with inimitable Parisian
class. A while back she had a punk party at New
Jimmy's, where she served beef stew in dog dishes and
chocolate mousse in a toilet bowl. What a laugh! And
then some real punks crashed the party and started
fighting with the fashionable pseudopunks and Regine
had to call in the real police to break it up and the
whole affair just thrilled her to death.

Talking of death. There's been a big Dracula
craze going on for the past several years. Dracula societies are flourishing, books and movies about the Tran-
sylvanian terror proliferate, and Andy Warhol, who, of
course, is never out of step with the times, did a Drac
flick. Dracula novelties ("Frothing Blood Capsules.
Harmless. 25¢") keep the plebs entertained when

they're not playing the pinball machines, and over in England one of the kids' favorite ice creams is a concoction called Count Dracula's Deadly Secret ("Moonwhite ice cream concealed in black-as-night water ice. Drink one before sunset!")

In his current acute undeadness, therefore, the Count is able to provide something for everyone. Even the terrorists have got in on the act. Back in 1974, the Peronist Montañeros, having killed Argentina's President Aramburu four years earlier, snatched his body from a Buenos Aires cemetery in an action called "Operation Dracula." And, in New York, there are currently two Dracula plays thrilling packed houses. (Two more folded in the same season after short runs.)

Regine is not one to ignore a trend. Punk's a drag now, she thinks, and so her latest party was a big Drac bash for the Beautiful People in the Big Apple.

As if rising from the inferno, they climbed through billowing clouds up the staircase to the ballroom, where artful spiderwebs hung overhead and glittering bats revolved in tight circles above the revelry. "You don't know how much I love you," the huge speakers blasted out as the night got under way.

They came by the score, decked out in varying combinations of red, black, and white, expensively shaped, for the most part, to evoke only the most exquisite horror. Masks and fangs and capes and wicked-looking makeup for those in sympathy with the devil; and the most susceptible innocence for the victims.

Everyone was supposed to be there, Regine's assistant told me that night. Mick and Rudi and Ursula Andress and Eartha Kitt and Patricia McBride and the

Ambassador of Iran to Morocco and Edward Villella and Egon von Fürstenberg and Melba Moore and Shelley Hack, whoever that is, and, of course, Andy, and even Louis Malle, and the Duke of Marlborough and his duchess.

The Beautiful People are—well, "beautiful" is the only word for it. There were some exceptions, to be sure. His Grace of Marlborough is not beautiful, and the Churchillian strain in his blood, which might have compensated, seems depleted by now. Angela Lansbury, if that was indeed she, looked ferocious enough to send Dracula yelping all the way back to Transylvania. A lesbian couple dancing smack-bang in the middle of the floor seemed about as chic as bartenders at Bonnie and Clyde's, which is probably what they were. And a man with plastered-down, wavy ash-blond hair looked all too much as though he could have been wearing black, red, and white for real forty years ago. The woman he was with was dressed in black, was *very* fat and ugly, and included so much real or feigned malevolence in her gestalt that she looked like a wrestler in drag.

But with these exceptions, the folk here were astonishingly beautiful. Across the room one lovely—his sex remained indeterminate until he came within earshot—was wearing white ballet tights and ballet shoes and a black peasant's shirt belted at the waist, and long earrings which dangled from his little lobes. His eyes were heavily mascaraed, and there were mascara fang marks on his slender neck. Oh, what a pale, sweet creature he looked as he tiptoed through the crowd, anxiously, incessantly searching for—was it the Count himself?

And the women! So many of such sheer beauty that one didn't even notice either Ursula or Eartha, though no one is saying they weren't there. Probably they just got lost in this crowd. With so much pulchritude, you couldn't help wondering what Paris would have done here with his apple: At a conservative reckoning, the average here was close to eleven hundred millihelens. Maybe, just maybe, Paris would have given it to that absolutely delightful creature who does the Charlie perfume commercials on TV, because her smile is like a thousand pearls even as she is deeply absorbed in a discussion with a girl friend about who is going to sleep with whom, or who has slept with whom, or something like that (I admit I eavesdropped a bit).

It was a smash party all right, even if it couldn't be expected—as a semipublic affair—to match the one given by the German millionaire Gunther Sachs in 1974 to celebrate his fortieth birthday. Roman and Elsa and Marissa were among the guests then, and the high point of the evening's fun and games that night in St. Moritz was reached when four statuesque blonds, naked except for jackboots to keep their little feet warm, marched in to Wagnerian music carrying a coffin, out of which fell a bloodstained hand. *Such* horror! *Such* decadence!

It is churlish, no doubt, to interrupt these revelries by recalling that Dracula is a hero drawn from real-life history. He was formally known as Prince Vlad, but even in his lifetime came to be called Count Dracula, that being the name for "dragon" among the

Walachian people over whom he ruled. He was also nicknamed "Tepes," or "Impaler."

By any standards, Vlad was a mass murderer, but he would have scorned the technological advances employed by his more recent emulators. His entertainment was to do things like impaling people on stakes and, if accounts are to be believed, chopping off their hands at the wrist and collecting their blood in huge copper caldrons. Sometimes he would drink the blood neat; but when hungry, he would add some soup to it. Toward the end of his career, it is said, he began to go more directly to the source by biting into the jugular veins of women.

To solve his kingdom's social-welfare difficulties, Vlad on one occasion summoned all orphans, widows, beggars, cripples, and other marginal individuals to his palace and, after providing them with a generous meal, did them all to death. In one account, he had them battered to death by his servants and threw their corpses to the wild bears and wolves which it was his pleasure to keep in a private zoo; according to another account, he simply had them all burned alive.

These barbarities occurred five hundred years ago, it is true. Nevertheless, it seems extraordinarily inappropriate—not to say tasteless—to celebrate this mass murderer as a folk hero. Would we take kindly to the idea of our descendants, half a millennium hence, festooning their pleasure domes with Auschwitz props and making a Hitler night of it?

The mind boggles at the prospect. The naked Aryan women would be there again, in their jackboots, of course; and perhaps the guests could travel in freight cars (how quaint!) to the Regine's of the day. Once there, they could titillate themselves by writhing in a make-believe gas chamber to the violent cadences of Hitler's speeches.

To be sure, the historical Dracula has been transformed into a vampire. (Prince Vlad's palace at Tîrgoviste, though, has now been made a tourist attraction, replete with a store selling memorabilia, by the resourceful Rumanian authorities: the latest thing in socialist realism, no doubt.)

In his modern guise, Dracula is part of the larger mythology of vampirism—in fact, its most familiar symbol. What does vampirism, à la Dracula in particular, hold out for people today? The question elicits some astonishing answers.

Here, for instance, are the thoughts of Professor Devendra P. Darma, of Dalhousie University in Nova Scotia, on the matter. "Modern civilization," he told guests at a dinner of the Dracula Society, "consists of the living dead. Why then should we object to the dead living? And the final message of Dracula is that 'nothing dies, and Life is Eternal.' "

This kind of exegesis is bound to have limited appeal. No matter; here's another suggestion about what Dracula means to us today. It comes from Daniel Farson, grandnephew of Bram Stoker, who wrote the original *Dracula*. "The vampire is bisexual," he writes. "He loves and bites indiscriminately. Though he (and often she) seems to favor the throats of young girls, no one is safe."

Well, that didn't help clarify things very much, either, so I went and spoke with David Richmond, a

has the stake hammered through his heart. In fact, given his cunning and general appeal, it is quite possible that he is not really dead anyway. "Aha!" Richmond said triumphantly. "How do you know he's not going to be reborn?" That might be a hope if we really liked Dracula, which, in fact, we have no genuine reason to do—only the authors' insistence that we should. But it certainly is inconsistent with the theology: Antichrist cannot survive his destruction if it is to be redemptive.

What we have here is not the good old plot of the forces of light against the forces of darkness, or even its antithesis, "Let's all be gung-ho for the devil." True, in this play we are more for the devil than for the good guys, but that's more a result of arbitrary rigging than of anything else.

What we end with, in fact, are the blahs—an intellectually confused and emotionally limp version of the doctrine that nothing matters. Or, in Richmond's terms: "Ultimately, perhaps, good and evil are equal." That is intended as a moral judgment, if you will, not just a quantitative one.

The reasoning behind this goes as follows, according to Richmond. Our society is one in which falsity and wickedness flourish. No authentic values bind us to one another anymore, there is no peer censure, and all that is left is the pressure, virtually from birth, to resemble your television set, because almost everyone else does. Richmond told me of a speech that was in the original script but that was truncated during rehearsal because it was "too political." Van Helsing, Dracula's nemesis, has been chiding the Count about his wicked ways. The Count's reply is quite simple.

With all the wars that have taken place, with the social, psychological, and physical carnage caused by the industrial revolution, with all the callousness that's part of everyday life, who is Van Helsing to say that Dracula should stop being a sucker?

There are, it seems, no innocents left. And so there is no reason to suppose that the world will be either better or worse off if Dracula disappears from it. In fact, put the fellow into elegant clothes, give him a sense of humor and bumbling, unattractive opponents, and you might even find some reason to wish he would stick around. The trite, undiscriminating moral indignation of this posture is no more convincing or interesting than the calcified dualism ("good and evil are equal") which has ostensibly emerged from it. Richmond's sympathy for the devil may be heartfelt—no doubt that is what it is all about—but it lacks substance, ingenuity, and reason.

Here are some other observations on Dracula as he appears in recent sources: He is terrifying, naturally: powerful, vicious, and in other ways much as we would expect him to be; but at the same time he has rather distinctive qualities, too. His assaults are entirely unpredictable, and defense against them is further undermined by the fact that he is unidentifiable, since he can assume any number of possible guises. A comic strip describes his attributes in the following fashion: "Now, my friends, let me elaborate for you some of the terrible supernatural powers a vampire has. Count Dracula, from sunset to sunrise, has the strength of twenty men. He throws no shadow and shows no mirror image. To hide himself he can command fog, storm, and thunder. He can change into a wolf, bat, owl, even a moth. He can vanish entirely, grow huge, or very tiny. Thousands of vicious rats answer his silent summons. Of course, he can see in the dark . . ."

Also noteworthy: In some versions, Dracula not only becomes an object of compassion but actually rises to the status of superhero. *Dell Comics* has a Dracula who, with his beautiful assistant, Fleeta, does battle against the forces of evil, very much in the spirit of Superman or Captain Marvel. Or, we might say, very much in the spirit of Batman, whose persona has obvious enough vampiric overtones.

Dracula, then, is protean. Both physically and morally he can become anything; which, in turn, also means that he lacks commitment to any form or purpose other than his own unliving, undead survival. He can be a dandy or a wolf, a hero or a villain. Are we drawn to him because of his seemingly limitless pliability of being?

5/Stool Angst

PUNK FURNITURE? HOW IN JOHNNY ROTTEN'S name can furniture be punk? It's got to be a gimmick, I told myself—just some opportunist cashing in on the moment's fad. But I marveled, nevertheless: punk *furniture?* What will they think of next?

Yet Richard Mauro has what might today pass for a serious philosophy. He objects to modern furniture on two grounds. One, when you plop yourself down on or at it, you don't really notice it; you just take it for granted. And two, much of the furniture that is around today is morally and aesthetically revolting, such as the fake Chippendale chairs you see, or those vinyl covers some people put over their upholstery.

Reasonable enough as a starting point, you might say, but where does the punk fit in? Well, Richard also believes that we should recycle our industrial debris, an idea he traces back to Charles Jencks's book *Adhocism: The Case for Improvisation.* Moreover, Richard is fascinated by banal, mass-produced industrial objects, such as safety pins and zippers.

Put all this together and what do you get? Well, it could be an ottoman made of a 150-yard-long industrial zipper sewn to itself in widening circles. Or a chaise that's an old army blanket completely covered by one thousand No. 3 safety pins. Or another ottoman, whose silver vinyl upholstery is stuffed with a mass of broken plates that Richard bought for a penny apiece on the Bowery. Or again, an ottoman filled with newspapers contained in the transparent vinyl your grandmother uses to protect her sofa.

All very satirical, no? And very chic, too, if you consider the $3,000-dollar price tag for the safety-pin number, or the $2,500 the zipper ottoman will set you back.

But there's more to all this than just satire. For one thing, the designs are actually rather attractive. They are nice to look at and not at all the kind of objects you would feel embarrassed to have around the house. But while Richard is happy they are this way, he insists that they are actually "paradigms of humor, surprise, sensuality, and fear."

Fear?

Yes. Yes: fear. And that's what makes them truly punk, you see. Take the plate-filled ottoman, for example. You sit on it, you hear the crockery crumble underneath you, and then—the *angst* hits you.

"What if I get jabbed in the ass?" You can't help asking the question even if Richard assures you beforehand that there is really no way the dishes can puncture the cover.

Or the safety-pin chaise. Its texture is wonderfully lustrous, and your impulse is to run your hands over it before sitting down. But even before you begin doing that the *angst* hits you again. What if one of the pins bursts open? Even this thought crosses your mind: "What if I sit on the thing and all the pins beneath me open and perforate my tush with hundreds of No. 3 holes?"

"It can't happen," Richard says. "It takes a hundred and twenty pounds of direct pressure to open a pin!" No doubt. But do you *really* believe him?

That, one might say, is the point. The humor and surprise and sensuality are all very well and good, but the fear and trembling at three grand for the privilege is what Mr. Mauro seems really to have on his mind.

Why? Is it because he's mad at us for not paying enough attention to the furniture we use? His way of getting us to sit up and take notice of what's important to him but taken for granted by us? Or is he expressing his contempt for anyone dumb enough to buy his merchandise—as though you deserved a bit of anxiety if you were willing to shell out three grand for his safety pins? (That's three bucks per pin!)

Richard's intention of getting us to pay more heed to furniture is fair enough. We should notice our furniture, our environment altogether, rather more than we tend to. However, there are many ways in which a furniture designer could go about getting us to do that—humor, surprise, and sensuality among them. In fact, the furniture could even be beautiful.

We would notice it in that case, too.

Why, then, does Richard try to evoke anxiety, and fear, as *his* way of getting us to pay attention?

To get an answer, I went to his enviably elegant and spacious loft on the edge of Brooklyn Heights. He wasn't wearing a safety pin in his ear or a blood-dripping swastika T-shirt or anything like that, and in general he seemed like a rather charming and intelligent young man—he is thirty-one—capable of showing very good taste.

I was struck, though, by the little witticism that first graced my encounter with him. Richard lives with a lady whose last name begins with "S." His last name, of course, begins with "M." To discourage burglars, he doesn't give the two names on the doorbell downstairs, but calls himself an "alarm company." The name of the alarm company? You guessed it: "S & M Alarm Company."

I asked him about punk, first of all. "I enjoy hearing about the violence in it, as everyone does," he replied. "Punk is the metamorphosis of what's happening in our society. Perhaps because we're not too involved in war anymore, or that kind of violence, and the press has to pull this kind of stuff on us to make us really stand up and take notice."

"What's so enjoyable about violence?" I asked. "Why is *that* the way to get people to sit up and take notice?"

"It's part of human nature, of course," he answered. "It's part of civilization."

"Sure. But isn't it one of the less attractive parts? One of civilization's objectives is to repress this kind of drive, and I would have thought that, in general, it's a good idea for the individual to repress them as well. And similarly with fear and anxiety. Civilization helps shield us from them, and individual growth is in good measure associated with learning how to overcome, or at least contain, them . . ."

"That's not true at all," Richard cut in vigorously. "Society has always been based on fear. Look at Nazi Germany. Look at Czarist Russia. Look at the United States until recently. Civilization is violence!"

By way of illustrating his point, he went over to his study and brought out a walking cane. "Look at this!" he said triumphantly. "You probably can't imagine what it's made of!"

After a short examination I acknowledged that I was stumped. With great pride Richard informed me that it was a stretched bull's penis—a bull's pecker, as he called it. The cane was used to whip people, probably slaves, during the eighteenth century, and Richard took care to call my attention to one part where it was rather worn. "You can see where it is worn away here, where they hit people with it. Isn't that beautiful?" And he went on to speculate that the dark stains on the cane were from blood.

"Collecting this kind of thing is my hobby," he told me.

I asked Richard again whether he thought it desirable to express our violence. He dithered around on this one for a while. "I feel our society has given up sexuality as well as violence," he said at one point, adding that he enjoys standing on the street talking to people while holding his bull's pecker between his legs.

Next, he talked about the need to vent the frustration we all feel. He mentioned that from time to time he throws chairs across the room, and that once he even hurled a $400-dollar watch against the wall. "Expressing violence is OK," he added, "but not to the point of hurting people."

I reminded him that the cane he so enjoys was used to hurt other people, *and* that he rather relished that fact—bloodstains and all. "That's true," he said, "but the cane is no longer used for that, that's over with. And, what's more, I don't practice violence myself, except on inanimate things like watches, chairs—that kind of thing."

"Why don't you," I asked, "seeing that you're co-owner of the S & M Alarm Company, and all?"

"Perhaps I'm too uptight," he replied. By way of illustrating the point, he mentioned that he was once invited to a party in downtown Manhattan. "Party" is the wrong word for the event; it was a sadomasochistic jamboree, really, to which people came from all over the world, although you had to be invited by one of the regulars.

Anyway, Richard was invited and he went. Almost at the outset of the proceedings, a man and his wife got up on the stage; the man tied the woman up, and bellowed at her, "Who am I?"

"My master!" she whimpered.

"And what do you deserve?"

"That you beat me!" was the reply. Which, of course, the master/husband proceeded to do until the woman's naked body was bleeding from the lashes of her man's whip. After a while, he invited a member of the audience to take over the job, and soon there was a long line of volunteers waiting their turn to whip and fuck the lady.

These celebrations, apparently, continued over a couple of days, and an excrutiatingly good time was had by all.

Except for Richard. Bull's pecker or no, he found the whole scene more than he could stomach, and after a while he left the party feeling quite disgusted and sickened.

Hoping, perhaps, to change the subject, I asked him to tell me about his life before he became a punk-furniture designer.

He was happy to do so. When he was a kid, Richard told me, he had wanted to become a neurosurgeon. He spent much of his spare time dissecting sheep's brains, and on one occasion removed a frog's gall bladder so successfully that the creature survived the operation. His family physician was very impressed by this, and, to encourage Richard, gave him the dissecting kit his father had given him when he went to medical school.

By the time he left high school, however, Richard decided that he wished to cure more than the merely temporal ills that physicians treat; he wanted to save souls from their propensity for eternal damnation. So he decided to become a priest.

"That's a pretty sadomasochistic thing," he said with a hearty laugh. "You've got to be really weird to want to become a priest!"

"How so?" I asked.

Richard explained that one of his spiritual advisers in the seminary gave him a cat-o'-nine-tails to help him learn how to emulate some of the early saints. He was a diligent student, and practiced on the instrument with enthusiasm—frequently to the point where blood was streaming down his back.

After about a year of this, however, Richard decided that he now liked himself better, so he gave up both his whip and the novitiate. He had a curious item of gossip on this matter, which is passed on here for those who are interested in this kind of thing. Nowadays, it seems, pious flagellants no longer use leather whips but flails made from hemp. They are not only a lot cheaper, but hurt less than the leather ones. "Priests aren't fools!" Richard remarked with his hearty laugh.

Turning again to the contemporary scene, Richard expressed his contempt for terrorists. "They're bullshit!" he said bluntly. "Let them attack a military post or police or something like that, and I could respect them. But a planeload of tourists, or a busful of children—defenseless people: That's disgusting. Terrorists are not serious people. They just want attention."

He was adamant on the subject and continued an eloquent denunciation of terrorism for several minutes until I interrupted to ask whether there was not a certain paradox in his remarks.

That is, he is against terrorism and accuses terrorists of wanting to get attention. Yet he himself tries to arouse terror in people who want nothing more than to sit down and feel comfortable in a chair. In a similar fashion, I continued, he is no longer into flagellation and walks out of the year's biggest S & M bash, yet enjoys going around with his bull's pecker and pointing out the bloodstains on it.

These remarks appeared to make Richard uncomfortable. He talked rapidly, made lots of funny jokes, and about five minutes later said, with a laugh, "I've gotten away from your question!"

I said that I had noticed that too, but before I had a chance to repeat the question, he said, "You know, I'm so blocked right now on this that if you were to ask me to tell you what the question was, I don't think I could." So I described the paradox again, and asked him to resolve it. He said that he couldn't.

"Might it be," I suggested, "that you're a kind of closet terrorist? Terrorists attack innocent people in order to get them to sit up and take notice of them. Isn't that what you are trying to do with your furniture?"

"Where's the paradox in that?" he asked.

"Well, let me put it this way," I offered. "Reik suggests that what the sadomasochist welcomes is not the pain—after all, that *hurts!*—but the fact that it enables him to feel *something,* and pain is the only thing which can make him feel.

"Could it be," I continued, "that you are in a sense both types of furniture: the kind that doesn't feel anything because it is all phony and encased in vinyl or whatever; and the kind that can only evoke feeling by the threat of violence and pain?"

Richard responded again with a flood of irrelevant, quick-fire witticisms, but after a while he told me of the bondage chair he had designed, and showed me a photograph of it.

We changed the subject again. "Why has punk come along at this particular time?" I asked.

"There are two reasons," he replied, without hesitation. "People are bored with themselves, with the news, with everything in general; everything feels bland and redundant. That's one reason: We need something to get us going. And the other's that there's been this duality for so long which the kids are seeing through, because they are fed up with it. The duality between public politeness and the kinds of rude profanities you use in private, for example. Let me bring all that violence out instead of hiding it: That's the kind of thing the kids are saying to themselves, and the press is helping them bring it out because it needs sensationalism. So punk is a way of attacking hypocrisy, really . . ."

Downstairs, as he was showing me out, Richard looked a bit bashful. "Could you just tell me that paradox again—you know, about the two kinds of furniture? I've already blocked it out."

6/ Studio 54, and Objects of Obscure Desire

IT'S A FAR-OUT SCENE IN THERE, THEY SAY about Studio 54, New York's inmost night spot. Money and squalor . . . punk and elegance . . . celebs and just plain beautiful folk. Andy stops by three or four times a week. Bianca has parties there. So does Liza. Jacqueline Bisset comes in every night when she's in town.

54 is the Grand Central of on-time trends, the spot where everyone comes to do his own thing no matter whether it's straight or gay or in-between or autosexual or menage-ing à trois or anything else you can think of. Excitement. Shock. Thrill. That's what 54 is all about. The General Assembly of weirdness and glamour, but without a Security Council to call things to a halt. A living, dancing, doping fantasy market where the one word that's not allowed is "no." A laboratory for probing the outer limits of who we are. "I don't care if a guy

who comes to the door is a multimillionaire," owner Steve Rubell says, "but if he looks like he'll be deadwood inside the club, we don't want him."

Once you're inside, though, they say you'll see that people are the greatest show on earth. Not to mention the brutal, throbbing rhythm of the world's most elaborate sound system, the jabbing lights, the rolling colors, the astounding props that cost a million dollars, the twice-nightly snowstorm of glittering polyethylene, and a rain show of colored balloons. And all this in the studio where "Name That Tune," "Your Hit Parade," and "The $64,000 Question" were once telecast.

Everything is happening here, but one thing is happening more than the rest—today's thing more than any other. For 54 is the beachhead of violence.

"The lights are vertical cylinders framed in columns of steel like *Star Wars* laser beams," one reads; and in case you miss the point, flashing police lights circle the base of each.

The door has been torn off the "subterranean Gothic closet of fetish clothing," *The Soho Weekly News* discloses. Chains, black leather, feathers, velvet, and lace—not to mention Nazi uniforms—have tumbled out of it in wanton profusion, only to be reassembled on the floor of 54: "the habits of nuns, the robes of priests and monks, the clothes of construction workers, firemen, and military, along with S & M gear and women in garter belts and corsets who look as if they'd stepped out of a Richard Lindner painting."

Not since Berlin in the twenties has there been such a scene; and even then the shuddering delight of fear was not throbbed on, as it is now, by the huge sound, the blinding lights "A storm trooper from *Star Wars* visited Studio 54 last night" *(New York Post)*. Fabulous Grace Jones, black and in black leather, a mean-looking whip in her hand and flanked by two black panthers, belts out her hit song, "I Need a Man!" What a hit! What a belt! The Night of the Locust! . . . "John Schlesinger didn't have it this easy when he filmed that final hysterical sequence for *The Day of the Locust:* The opening night of 54 was probably more frightening" *(Daily News Record)*. Wow! Gotta get there!

But you can't walk in—even if you are not a deadwood multimillionaire. The press agent will arrange a visit, however. Friendly Ed gives a fluid rap about the scene. He doesn't quite call it Xanadu, but that it's the ultimate in pleasure, in freakiness, in trendiness becomes entirely apparent from the very beginning of his pitch.

Only at one point did Ed's press-agent smoothness give way—and then to an equally effortless, rapid-fire display of a country auctioneer's insults. I had asked who the Kubla Khan of all this splendor and excitement was.

"Who?" Ed asked with an incredulity that was at once genuine, outraged, and mocking. *"Who?* You a man from Mars or something? You never heard of Steve Rubell? Ask any cabdriver in town who Steve is! He's the most famous man in town!"

We became friends again after I asked Ed how Mr. Rubell's name was spelled; an invitation followed to visit the office and go through the mountain of press clippings about Studio 54. "Only don't call it a nightclub. It's a disco," Ed cautioned. "We don't have any of the polyester-double-knit crowd from New Jersey here, you know!" I promised to remember that.

I wondered about Ed, the Ron Ziegler of Chicgate today. His voice and intonation on the phone indicated that he was definitely not a young man. And his manner, tough and rasping, seemed about as sleek and far-out and now and pulsating with sinuous excess as a Rotary Club luncheon speaker in Ramapo. I also wondered, idly, whether he wore polyester double knits.

Ed was out when I arrived to look at the clippings, but there was a certificate from the Brooklyn College Alumni Association, inscribed to what appeared to be another member of his family, hanging on a wall. So perhaps it wasn't Ramapo after all. The clippings I looked at echoed Ed's rap confirming (or was it just a coincidence?) its authenticity. One item, though, caught my eye. A promotional blurb sent out before 54's opening described the fantasy palace as "a *déjà vu* look into the future!"

And now the big night arrived. "The scene only gets moving after twelve," Ed cautioned. "It'll be an exciting night. None of the double-knit crowd," he added, possibly as a reminder.

A large crowd thronged outside the door. None of them would get in. "I've heard that spiel about leaving your cards at home every night this year, ten times a night," one of the bouncers called out with a contemptuous tone that evidently goes down well with his audience. "But unless I see a card, none of you's gettin' in!" The crowd did not disperse. They were at the gateway to the shrine, and that was as far as they would get. No matter, evidently: Some of the charisma would rub off. "I was at 54 last night and I . . ."

Ed's name worked wonders. Like Moses parting the Red Sea, the bouncers cleared a way for us and—we were in! A Japanese girl in a kimono sat by the inside door collecting tickets: very exotic despite her midwestern accent. Turns out that Ed's name got us past the front door, but not past the twenty dollars it was going to cost the two of us to get beyond the Oriental lady. The phone next to her rang. "Shit!" she said. "Bet it's another crank call." Seems that that night they had already received five bomb threats and an uncountable number of obscene calls. But that's not unusual, the girl told me.

Twenty bucks later we were standing in line at the hatcheck counter. "That'll be a dollar-fifty," the girl said coldly.

"In advance?" I asked in surprise.

She looked up for the first time. "Yes," she said, even more coldly.

"Hell, one doesn't even have to do that at Brew 'n Burger!" I protested, but she was already looking around for a bouncer, so I pretended it was a joke and left hurriedly.

Inside, the noise from the loudspeakers was stupendous—even the mid-range notes thumped painfully on my rib cage. Nevertheless, a lot of people were dancing to it, all very animatedly, some rather skillfully, and everyone seemed to be sweating a great deal.

The lights flashed on and off in a chain of puerile

sequences. An art-deco mountain appeared on the wall behind the dance floor and a few moments later was replaced by clouds drifting slowly across (quite incongruous, in their placidity, to the frenetic sounds, lights, movements all around), and then by a huge fence of multicolored punching bag–like objects. The whole thing felt a lot like one of those plop-plop-fizz-fizz commercials before the Alka-Seltzer has begun to work its benign effect. It was strongly irritating, that's all, and I would say that you had to be pretty gullible to find variety or pretty stoned (as a number of people seemed to be) to find excitement or significance in the shifting patterns of light and texture. They intruded, merely, by their persistence.

The vigor seemed quite phony, therefore, and devoid of substance. All in all, the place was about as enlivening as the end of *Love Story* is moving: It was the now equivalent of sentimentality.

And the people? Most probably they were not even plastic, but just ordinary folk who had somehow got past the door and were checking out the scene everyone's talking about. Nothing far-out, though, except for one man who looked Puerto Rican and had a black eye patch and a brassy bandolier-looking number across his chest. One woman was wearing an indubitably polyester-double-knit jump suit (sleeveless, admittedly), for which she was rather too fat, and whose rust color ill became her peroxide. But she was having a good time jumping up and down to the music, and within a couple of months' time the Studio 54 hype machine, having run out of grist, managed to make her into a temporary celebrity—the Grandma Moses of the disco scene. The beautiful girls were not all that many; more often than not they were not particularly elegantly dressed, and more often than not they were attended by gray-haired men in business suits who expressed the spirit of the times by unknotting their ties and hanging them around their necks, just as you can see in your local betting parlor. Altogether, the scene here seemed pretty chintzy compared with the folk over at Regine's—perhaps a bit like an Oshkosh idea of what Bloomingdale's looks like: strangely provincial.

A smashing chick, nice big, deep cleavage, pert nipples extruding just an inch or two below the neckline, was hugging her gray-haired man, nibbling on his earlobe as they do in the movies, and playing with his tie. He whispered something in her ear, she stepped back a couple of paces and began making like she was jerking him off. Giggling with delight, she looked around for approval, encouragement, perhaps just acknowledgment of what a funny, lively, audacious thing she was. No one else seemed to notice her, so I gave her a wan smile.

A stir of recognition—a celebrity! He was sitting on a sofa near the dance floor, one of the house's two-fifty drinks in his hand, and his face looked vaguely familiar. We couldn't quite place him, though. Was it the Alpo commercial? Or Lysol? He looked up, pleased to be recognized.

This really *is* a scene here. The place used to be a theater and still is. The dance floor is where the stage was, and the lights and all those expensive, futile props hang over it just as they do in a theater. And either because it would have been too costly to remove or because it really is an essential part of the scene, the old balcony, with twenty-seven tiered rows of movie-hall seats, has been left the way it was. So lots of people sit up there like a passive audience watching the scene below, which actually is so boring that most of them sustain their curiosity only by getting high on drugs.

"The show's the thing," the hype reports. "Public displays of sexual enticement and abandon replace one on one intimacy—perhaps a reflection of the cynical social trend toward general emotional distance. Doin' it on the floor of Studio 54 is where it's at for sex . . ." and so on.

If only it were true. But there's no show really, only Sartre's new hell: a crowd of voyeurs with not one exhibitionist, an audience of Fellini-goers trapped in a Doris Day special. One woman down there was dancing in quite wild abandon, a good sight. The very loose shoulder straps on her dress kept falling off. Each time the moment of danger impended, though, she stopped, adjusted her dress, and then returned to her gyrations. "Rich punks uptown like to show tits and ass," we're told. Bulldoodoo. They like to *see* it, natch. But there ain't no one here who's showin' it.

Indeed, this place just isn't sexy. No meat-market feeling to it at all, let alone a view of any of those gorgeous women caressing each other's breasts like you see in the glossies. No menacing excitement, either, not even leather and chains or swastikas. Only that creep with the bandolier over his chest.

A group of five real punks arrived. They were very young, acned, and kept close together, looking rather shy. One had a skull and crossbones painted on the nice leather of his jacket. All had Coor's beer cans in their hands. They walked around for five minutes or so, then left, fifty bucks the poorer among them.

Wending his way through the crowd was a burly, sandy-haired man who looked very much like an Irish cop on a family picnic—beige windcheater, green tartan pants. I headed toward him. "Hi there, Ed!" I called out. "I'm the man from Mars, remember? Glad to meet you at last!"

He didn't ask me how I recognized him. There was some haggling over the twenty bucks, but Ed was adamant and there was nothing to be done about that. Outside, the crowd had grown thicker. The people looked expectantly at us and then returned their attention to the bouncer's gibes. A long line of empty cabs waited for fares.

"What goes on in there?" the cabby asked.

"That, my friend," I replied, "*that* is the $64,000 question."

"You've gotta get me two memberships, Dave!" the man in the elevator pleaded with his friend as we were being lifted slowly up to the thirty-fourth floor of a mid-Manhattan office building.

It was a cat-and-mouse game, and the cat was loving every moment of it. "Gee, Frank," he said. "I'd love to, but . . ."

Frank cut in. "My friend is a real cool guy, you know. He's a great partier. His wedding was at *the Plaza!* It was just great." He paused, searching for more. "His dad's one of the biggest lawyers in town, you know, a hotshot in the Inner Circle."

The cat remained unimpressed. "So what?" he purred. "Steve is always complaining to me about how many of the polyester-double-knit, bagel-nosh crowd manage to get into 54."

"You mean Steve Rubell? You *know* him?" the mouse asked.

"Where's your friend from, anyway?" the cat replied, ignoring the question. "The Bronx?"

"No, of course not!" the mouse whined. "Listen, Dave, you gotta get us into 54. Please!"

"Ah, so he's not a BBQ?" the cat said. The mouse was caught off guard. "BBQ?" he asked. "What's that?"

"You see what I mean?" the cat said triumphantly as the elevator door slid open. "It stands for Brooklyn, the Bronx, and Queens—double-knit land. Gee, Frank. If you don't know that kinda thing, I just don't see how I'm going to get you into 54 . . ."

Only a few hours later, I got a phone call from Peter Beard. Peter was in town for a few days after skiing in Aspen, and would soon be returning to his home in Kenya. He had been highly recommended to me by Ed, the Studio 54 hypester, who said that Peter could teach me more about the scene there than anyone else. Ed said that even though Peter was a photographer, he was very anthropological, which seemed to me a splendid recommendation; and not long before Peter had had a big cover story in *The New York Times* magazine about dead elephants. A man who photographs dead elephants and is very anthropological could not be a total bore, I decided, and so I was very glad Peter had called.

He suggested that I come over and see him right away at the Westbury Hotel on Madison Avenue, where he was staying, and I said sure, it would only take about half an hour to get there. In fact, it took forty-five minutes, because of the Armed Forces Day parade, which closed off a lot of crosstown traffic. I rang the bell, and the door was opened by a very beautiful young lady with a French accent. She was a fiery-looking type with big black eyes and rich, curly black hair, and she was sort of covered by a much too large Yves Saint Laurent dressing gown, which was also black. She was very friendly and slightly shy, and it was with a very nice smile that she pointed out the bedroom in which Peter was. She followed me to the room and got into bed with Peter, who was naked except for a towel around his waist: and into bed, too, with the other young lady who was already there and who, at my approach, demurely covered her body with the sheet.

This other lady was also very beautiful and young, but rather more the svelte type, though further details were not only obscured by the sheet for most of the time, but by the large sunglasses she was wearing despite the fact that the room was lit only by two television sets—one black-and-white, the other color—that were both tuned in to the ABC evening news. Peter told me how to turn the sound off on the sets, and for most of the time I was there, the lady in the sunglasses continued to look at the noiseless pictures on the twin screens.

I should say, of course, that I have interviewed literally hundreds of celebs in bed with their two beautiful young ladies, and that I was therefore not in the least bit fazed by the setting here in the bedroom of Room 1112 of the Westbury Hotel. Besides, everyone was very friendly, even the lady in the sunglasses, and they encouraged me to sit on or right next to the bed and to take off my tie and jacket and so on, and the whole thing was cool—just entirely cool, and not at all distracting.

Peter is a very well preserved and handsome forty-year-old who is what they call a society figure and gives the impression, rightly or not, of having been born with a silver spoon in his mouth. He's written a number of books, each filled with his own photographs, and the latest is about how the wildlife experts in Kenya are destroying the species they're trying to preserve—not out of malevolence, of course, but because their humanitarian concern is most profoundly counterproductive.

We began by talking about punk because Carol, the lady in the sunglasses, who turns out to have been the obscure object of desire in Bunuel's latest flick, had just finished a punk movie. The guy in the movie, Peter explained, is just a stress victim of Stress City, and Carol is a French journalist, and they both get up to some pretty weird behavior. But Peter said that it's a very good movie, with a lot of S & M in it; and then he and Carol talked for a while about the need to change the movie's title, which I can't remember any longer but which apparently bears no relation to the movie itself. That thought led Peter to tell me that he loves the names of some of the punk groups: the Fuck Ups and the Disgustings are two he singled out for special mention. I asked him to tell me about Studio 54.

"I don't like the New York scene," he replied, "and I don't like 54 in particular. It's not very attractive, but to me New York is so unattractive I suppose 54 fits right into the picture. The only thing we've got left is anthropological horror. 54 is a theater of the apocalypse, the last dance, a real product of stress and density. I just end up there every night, I mean, because there's nothing like it in New York, not just because it goes on all night but because it's just like watching a rat colony. It's timely, appropriate, revolting. The people there are not in charge at all. They're very sick."

Cleo, the first girl, cut in to tell me what she thought the scene was all about—punk in particular. "It's a search for identity, really," she said with great rapidity and intensity. "Imagine the life they live, those poor kids, in these ghastly surroundings, skyscrapers and everything. Now, with punk, they've got something they can belong to. It's such a huge city. You don't belong to anyone, every race is mixed up, and suddenly they created punk and every kid has something to belong to, a reason to be. It's anarchy, totally; because they don't believe in anything, they just rebel against everything around them, and that's the only way they can express it."

"It's a cheap and vulgar world we're entering," Peter added, pronouncing the words with such unassailable authority that it seemed probable he had learned them on his grandfather's knees. "And there's plenty of violence in it," he continued. "New York has been on the verge of terrorism since the sixties. The black populations have been shifted and appeased at every emergency. Don't forget that's still going on.

They give 'em a little money so that they can breed a little more, and then there's a long, hot summer and they throw 'em a little more . . . They're reproducing like rats."

He turned back to the subject of Studio 54. "It's the best thing going, you know: the ultimate anthill. I don't think punk is appealing at all. It's a perversion, an end result. I'm not interested in trends, punk, fagotry. I used to do these diaries that focused on stress activities, but now the world is becoming a lot more stressful than even my diaries, and I just gave it up, there's no point continuing that kind of writing."

I asked what is so stressful about New York.

He repeated the question with mock incredulity. "The population densities, for one thing," he brought himself to explain, "and increased communications that allow all these declared wars and undeclared wars and controversies to reach us every morning in the newspapers and on TV. Of course this is an increasingly violent world! There's incredible violence in it! And the violence is nature's way of giving us a few warnings: Disease and war are the only way of keeping the densities down. But of course we're so fucking smart we'll find a way of getting around them and ultimately create a world that's no longer worth living in."

Carol, the lady in the sunglasses, muttered something about "the Blank Generation," which is a punk song; and Cleo, the other lady, picked up on the theme and, as intensely and rapidly as before, commented, "The Blank Generation! That represents everything to us. We know religions are absurd myths, that's all, for human control, convenience, whatever; and people are now looking for other things—flying saucers, ESP, astrology—but I don't really think they are going to find anything, and I don't even think they believe they are going to. So despair comes out. These people don't know what to do with themselves. It's a desperate search."

"Do *you* belong to the Blank Generation?" I asked her. But it was Peter who replied. "Of course not!" he said. "You don't take that kind of thing seriously. There's nothing serious about it. It's an indicator, a sort of barometer of the climate. Just walk around New York, that's all you have to do, to understand what's happening."

"And what do you see when you walk around New York?"

"Disease!"

"There are a lot of people here leading purposeful lives, wouldn't you say?" I asked.

"You're not being serious, are you?" Peter replied with palpable scorn and disbelief. "I see everyone on increasing drugs, increasing escapes of one kind or another. Everyone's trying to escape."

"It's the most desperate thing!" Cleo echoed, tightening the YSL dressing gown protectively around herself. "The world's absolutely desperate!"

"It *is*?" I inquired.

Peter added, "I went to some S & M activists' meetings with Larry Rivers. It was rather like gay activists, they wanted to bring the thing out into the open. You can't imagine all the things that are in the closet waiting to get out."

"All this is beginning to make you sound like you belong to that Blank Generation," I told him.

"I'm forty," he said in reply. "I'm still so purpose-lessly directed, I can look at anything and everything. If 54 was a place where people went to commit suicide, I'd still go there. In fact, I'd love to see that!"

"Why has sadomasochism come along as the re-course of the Blank Generation?" I asked.

"Perhaps it's guilt," he answered unhesitatingly. "With the curse human beings have put on the planet. I mean, we've absolutely wrecked the world wherever we've gone. I suppose the only way people can enjoy themselves is through their own punishment for being such destructive entities. I don't know . . . Maybe I'm wrong, but I've thought about it all a lot. We're living in a world where we can't experience genuine joy. Joy doesn't fit in, it's out of line for us. But genuine pain is more in line with what's happening. I find it rather appropriate."

"In what way is mankind so destructive?" I asked.

"Look at the world!" he said angrily. "Similariza-tion. Commercialization. False politics. Equalitarianist philosophies. All kinds of artificialities that human be-ings impose on the destruction they wreak. They're so out of touch with anything real. Way out of touch with anything real. And the Catholic church has probably perverted more people than almost anything I can think of except density."

"Density?" I asked, enjoying the chance to sound incredulous.

Peter explained the matter to me. We are breed-ing too many people. Not too many people for the world to feed, necessarily, but too many for us to be able to live with. The amount of space available to us is limited by the size of our globe, and there's nothing we can do about changing that, of course. So, to repeat, it's not a question of food but of space. Already, population densities are far in excess of what is acceptable, and this situation can be expected to deteriorate further. High densities derange us. The stress they engender leads to all the aberrant behavior that is taking place in the world. (This, by the way, is where the elephants fit in. Postmortems on elephants herded by the preservationists into fresh settlements showed that most of them were suffering from heart conditions brought about by the stress of living in unnaturally high densities. Beard regards the fate of these elephants as a premonition of what lies in store for us—indeed, of what is actually happening to us.)

Cleo, meanwhile, although nodding vigorously in agreement with everything Peter had been saying on the subject of densities, was now anxious to move from the sociological "they" to the confessional "I."

"I belong to the Blank Generation," she acknowledged. "I have no beliefs. I belong to no community, tradition, or anything like that. I'm lost in this vast, vast world. I belong nowhere. I have absolutely no identity. The bigger the population gets, the more difficult it is to communicate with anyone, and you're lost in this vast world of meaninglessness. It's all so meaningless. You don't even have family anymore. Punk is against everything. But, of course, it has no solution."

"So how do you cope with that?" I asked. *"Do* you cope?"

"The more aware you are," she told me, "the

more you're disgusted by it all and the more difficult it is to find enthusiasm and ambition. I look at art and people and society and it's all disgusting. The more you see of it, the less you want to belong to it."

"It's not a pose," Peter explained. "It's a density phenomenon. She's just trying to get through."

Carol asked him for another pillow, and he gallantly offered her one of his. I commented on the density problem in the bed, but no one seemed to think that was funny and they ignored my remark.

"We're in a screwed-up world," Peter continued once Carol was comfortably resettled. "The other day we were down in the Central Park Zoo watching the gorilla. The audacity of the human species to take these incredible animals and put them in the same prison we're in, and standing there like rock apes tuning in— but not tuning in, losing the whole point of not being able to see that there's us just a couple of million years ago!"

I didn't quite get this point myself, but Peter had now become very agitated and pressed on with his train of thought. "The Blank Generation is the one which can't bring itself to contribute to the American Cancer Society or to the Wildlife Fund and things like that which in the past had a certain amount of purpose and point. There isn't any point in contributing to bureaucracy: All you get are more bureaucrats. What's the point in programs for relieving starvation when we know more food means more people? What's the point in electing politicians when we're electing parasites who throw back in our faces what we want?"

Cleo interrupted to offer her exegesis. "We don't believe in what surrounds us, so why contribute to it? Before, people wanted to contribute, and to create. But why should anyone want to now?"

Peter's animation found a target in me. "What's it like to be a college professor?" he asked. "I can't believe anyone would even want to do their assignments. I wouldn't know what I'd be working my ass off for. I went up to Yale just the other day, and all you find up there is a completely wasted community. It was always pretty ugly, but now it's just garbage: shut-down theaters and hotels, and just a lot of bars full of blacks on welfare . . ."

He nodded in vigorous agreement when I asked whether this too is a density phenomenon. And as for teaching—I replied that I knew people, including some at Yale, who are searching for understanding and even for truth.

"Oh for God's sake!" Peter snapped impatiently, and turned around to snuggle with Carol.

"I'd rather be blind in this kind of world than find the truth!" Cleo echoed. "There's no pleasure in that! Truth is an absolute depressant!"

Peter broke off for a moment to add his own epigram. "The truth nowadays is somehow to find enough money to buy a boat and get out into the ocean."

"Oh, but I think there are plenty of people around who are not looking for *that*!"

"There are plenty of people around who are very limited, don't forget," Peter reminded me. "One of the first things we do is to delude our offspring, as R. D.

Laing points out. You get people young enough, and you can persuade them that what's going on is not going on."

"It would be so much easier if I were limited!" Cleo sighed in a most becoming way.

"You've only got one life, so your first duty is to yourself, to do something that's personally rewarding," Peter said. "I believe in selfishness. Benevolence: The road to hell is paved with it. It's just another way to create more problems."

"Is the blankness just temporary?" I asked. "What lies beyond it?"

"I don't think it's temporary," he replied. "I think it is a preview of coming attractions. Density demands a solution, and war, death, and disease are ahead. The future will be far more active, but it will be destructive action to prune the population. But the population is expanding beyond the possibility of meaningful limitation, I think. I'm amazed all college students aren't on drugs. It's all so futile, isn't it? Shockley and Jensen are the only ones who are interested in the number-one problem, and no one will even let them *talk*!"

"We've realized that progress is destruction," Cleo chimed in. "It's led us to nothing—nothing but the destruction of nature and human beings. And when you realize that, you go—blank."

"We don't care about anything," Carol contributed, her sunglasses still pointing at the two TV screens.

"Nothing?" I asked.

"It's like the Jews at Auschwitz," Peter answered for her. "You care about them being gassed, but you get into the same line with them. We're increasingly part of a downhill program that is in direct ratio to all the sentimental scapegoats that are invented to delude us into getting into deeper water . . ."

I was rather baffled by that one until Peter illustrated his meaning by pointing to the way the Jewish press Mafia—as he called it—had railed against Indira Gandhi when she went around India sterilizing men so they couldn't procreate. "They're running the media," Peter added, of the Jews. "Their humanitarian concerns sound marvelous, but they don't solve anything." That train of thought led Peter to say something about how our balance-of-payments problem is being exacerbated by the flow of dollars to Israel. I was not anxious to pursue this line to where I sensed it might be leading Peter, so I changed the subject.

"We're incapable, then, of solving our problems?"

"I think so. Definitely. Yes," he replied.

Just then the phone rang. "It's Suzy Chaffee," Cleo told Peter, with just a shade of resentment in her voice. I wondered whether the former Olympic skiing champion was on her way up to Room 1112 with a supply of Chap Sticks for the tremulous trio. But I didn't stay to find out. Heaven forfend that I should contribute further to the room's density. And the resultant stress.

7/Beat Me at Le Château 19

"EVERY TUESDAY AND THURSDAY AT 7:00 P.M., Château 19 invites you to a party. Nonprofessional demonstrations of sexual dominance and submission are featured," the flier reads. It goes on to promise: "Whenever possible, there will be prearranged real S & M scenes, presenting aspects of bondage, humiliation, discipline, piercing, etc. There will always be opportunities to meet others of similar interests during several hours of active socializing, when spectators and participants merge their roles. . . . Use of our custom-made stationary devices, including a bondage ladder and whipping horse, is free at all times. . . . Château 19 offers you S & M reality," the handout continues, mentioning among the establishment's other offerings "intimacy areas" and "free checkroom for costumes."

I found the Château in one of Manhattan's less

prepossessing districts, a lot of suburban-looking station wagons with New Jersey license plates parked outside. The club (it does double duty on other evenings as a meeting spot for "swinging couples") is only somewhat dingy, its bathrooms are clean, the service is polite and friendly, and, for those who can't quite get into the mood, distraction is available in the form of three exciting pinball machines. At a guess, two hundred people or so would fill the place to capacity.

At seven-thirty, when I arrived, about two dozen men and five women were already there. They looked —and were dressed—like your ordinary white, middle-class crowd and were sitting around alone or in small groups talking quietly, listening to the not very loud rock music that was coming out of the speakers, and sipping beer. With the exception of one elderly couple who seemed at least in their late sixties, the clientele ranged from mid-twenties to mid-forties.

Only one person was at all conspicuous, and he was very conspicuous indeed. Ritchie, I think his name was, was a kind of maître d'hôtel, bouncer, and ringmaster combined, though to look at him you would think he was a model for the Underground's catalogue —bedecked as he was in black leather, chrome, studs, belts, thongs, chains, boots, and handcuffs. He was also immensely burly, but despite all this, his manner was amiable and polite, and his face had the not enormously intelligent but nevertheless *distingué* and genial expression that in England, at least, one associates with Conservative party members of Parliament.

In the lower part of the split-level room, the bondage ladder and whipping horse promised in the house advertisement stood rather forlornly. A number of people sat on large cushions waiting for something to happen.

But nothing did happen for the next half hour or so. I picked up some of the literature from a table in the entrance hall and read it to pass the time. One item was a want ad. "SLAVES!" it read. "Fantasy Fulfillment Un-Limited is once again pioneering new areas for you. There are hundreds of potential Masters and Mistresses whose whips are just crying out for new slaves. Therefore, RENT-A-SLAVE is now taking applications from select men and women who are seeking Masters and Mistresses on a per diem, temporary or permanent basis. . . . Slaves are wanted to serve as masseurs, foot slaves, petticoat slaves, french maids, butlers, toilets, cooks, hairdressers, valets, fan bearers, house cleaners, little children, infants, chauffeurs, entertainment and sexual servants," and so on.

Another brochure advertised an "S-M Weekend" sponsored by Château 19, at $190 per couple. The event is to be held in a luxury hotel in upstate New York. Dress is casual, the brochure said; "Costumes are of course optional." There were also some items from the Eulenspiegel Society, "an S & M Liberation Group," one of which was a newsletter reporting the activities of chapters around the country.

All this seemed to fall a bit short of the "S & M reality" the flier had promised. The girl behind the bar told me that things would only liven up in a couple of hours, so I went out, had a leisurely dinner, and returned for the reality.

Lots more station wagons with New Jersey license plates were parked outside when I got back; indoors, the place was full, but not unpleasantly packed. In the whole crowd, perhaps ten people were dressed for the occasion, although none could rival Ritchie's apparel. In fact, a number of the dressers made only token concessions to the scene. One man, for example, still looked very much the conservative lawyer in his pin-striped suit and white shirt, but he had removed his necktie and placed in its stead a black leather, chrome-studded collar, which, to say the least, did not really seem to go with his outfit. Another man had placed a similar band around his wrist; for the rest, he remained very much the professional man with formal suit and white shirt.

Then the action began. A young man with shoulder-length blond hair announced that Mistress Nan was going to teach someone a lesson or two, and asked if there were any volunteers. People crowded round to watch, but no one volunteered, and Mistress Nan made a few surly remarks that did nothing to produce a student for her. Presently, however, a young black man stepped forward, took off a nicely cut dark-gray suit, a rather offensive light-blue Qiana shirt, BVDs, socks, and shoes, and was then trussed up with all sorts of chains and thongs by Mistress Nan. She placed him on the ladder, she placed him on the whipping horse, she made him go down on all fours, she made him lick her boots, and periodically she whipped him with a Lucite-handled number across the back and bottom. The young black man was completely obedient, didn't move except when she told him to, didn't say anything because his mouth was gagged, and, to tell the truth, seemed to be as bored by the whole procedure as every-one else was. And you can't really say it was a whipping that he got, because a fly-swatter would attack his prey with at least three times the vigor that Mistress Nan generated. But there was nothing else to do, so most people stayed around and watched, and someone made a remark to the effect that this must be one of the clips that they edited out of the TV version of *Roots* because it was too dreary.

Behind me, I sensed some movement. Turning around, I saw that about twenty people had formed a semicircle in front of Ritchie, who was sitting on a sofa with a young lady. Aha! I thought, perhaps some real action now. And evidently the same thought occurred to still more people, because in the few moments before I joined the group, it had grown considerably. But all it really amounted to was Ritchie sitting on the sofa with the young lady, and after a while, so that no one would feel too bad, he put his hand on her breast (she was fully clothed), and that was as far as this spectacle went.

I headed for the bar. A girl walked by, relatively attractive, and the man next to me said to her in a very sexy voice, "Hi there!" She stopped and turned to give him a smile, whereupon he said, real serious-like, "You come here to have a *terrible* time?" Her smile froze as his blossomed, and then his froze when she said, "You're a dumb jerk!" and walked away.

Presently, a man who looked like Robert McNamara, only about fifteen years younger and twenty pounds heavier, walked out. He held a chain in one hand, and at the other end of the chain was a most extraordinary sight. Specifically, a very fat, probably middle-aged man, naked except for his white socks and the jungle of chains and straps by which his arms were bound behind his back. One couldn't tell much more about him because his entire head was covered with what seemed to be a very tight-fitting black leather mask. The McNamara-like man was nice to him, however, guided him so that he wouldn't bump into things, and led him to a small circle of friends, who took turns beating him with a leather whip. Old No-Face took this punishment like a man, which is not surprising, because no one really hit him at all hard, except when a woman once did, which led everyone to say, "No, no, that's too hard," for which she apologized. Then his mentor led him to a sofa, laid him face up on it, and abandoned him to his fate.

But that couldn't have been too terrible, since the lady who had apologized for hitting him too hard came and sat down next to him and patted his shoulder gently from time to time. It's amazing what one can get used to, really, because in no time at all I came to regard this bizarre sight as simply part of the environment, and everyone else seemed to also and paid no attention to him.

Except for a young lady who threw a glass of beer at him. This caused his lady friend to get very upset. She called Ritchie, and they both told her that she had no right to do that because "he doesn't belong to you!" The malefactor was defiant, however, and proclaimed to all and sundry that she had just acted out the fantasy of each and every one of us, which I really don't think was at all the case.

Back at the whipping horse, Mistress Nan had procured another student and was working him over, too, in her inimitably desultory fashion. Presently, she was joined by Mistress Terror, but even this addition failed to increase the voltage. The new student looked as bored as his fellow, and the audience looked even more bored and unable for the most part to escape because the place was by now too crowded to permit much movement.

I squeezed past to a side room which had been divided into three cubicles by shoulder-high partitions. In two of these, spectators and participants had merged their roles, to quote from the flier: that is, people were thrashing each other. The cubicles were filled with onlookers, who were as bored, and with as good reason, as those watching Mistress Nan and Mistress Terror.

Even the two free bottles of Tuborg that came with my seven-fifty admission fee were doing nothing to relieve the sense of tedium. I caught sight of Ritchie, who was also looking pretty bored. He went over to a lady, who evidently was known to him, and took her clothes off. This caused a temporary flutter of excitement, which passed when the indelicacy of the physique he was uncovering became fully apparent. Ritchie took the lady down to the bondage ladder—which is actually only a stepladder with rings on its sides to which you can fasten chains and thongs or whatever else you fancy.

Nan and Terror's students were told to put their clothes on, which made everyone grateful, although the more recent student proved a bit intractable by insisting on licking Terror's boots, which she did not seem to mind too much. Terror, though, had other things on her mind and began fondling the new woman's breasts while Ritchie smacked the latter's behind. Then Ritchie climbed up the ladder behind the lady and kissed her while a person who can only be described as a transsexual in drag began fellating the lady. Presently, he gave way to Mistress Terror, who administered a few strokes of the whip (but really very softly) to the lady's private parts; and she in turn gave way to a man in priest's robes who rubbed his cane in the same area.

But nothing came of this at all, and soon the demonstration disintegrated into a lot of confusion, which was only heightened when the McNamara-looking man brought No-Face down to the demonstration area and made him stand there.

All the while—throughout the entire evening, that is—the rock music continued to play out of the speakers. It bore no relation to the action taking place, just as, of course, the action itself bore no relation to the wicked fantasies which, presumably, had brought people here: "Château 19 offers you S & M reality."

"Have you ever used a wheel?" I heard one man ask another as I was leaving. "No," his companion replied. "I've heard about them, though." "Yeah," the first man said. "I haven't used one either."

Outside, a man walked up the street with me to his car. "That place is full of shit," he said angrily.

"I think it's rather interesting," I replied.

"I think it's full of shit," he insisted.

"So do I," I explained. "That's why I find it interesting. Is there any other place around where more goes on?" I asked.

"Nah," he replied. "This is the only one."

"Well," I said, "that's probably just as well, don't you think?"

I discussed Château 19 with Jerzy Kosinski, the novelist, who appears to know the place better than I, and who had been recommended to me by a number of people as a man who has a lot to say about sadomasochism.

He told me about a man he had once met—I think it was in Château 19—who had come to New York on a short trip from the Midwest, where he lived and operated a large trucking outfit or something like that. The man was somewhat grossed out by what he saw in Château 19 and, because he recognized Kosinski's face, went over and talked to him for a while so that he would not be alone and unable to cope with the action.

Some months later, Kosinski ran into the man again quite by chance. They went and had a cup of coffee, and the man told him how his life had been changed. It seems that he used to pinch his girl friend's breasts quite hard, an innocent enough pastime and one which, although unusual, gave both of them much pleasure. This was all that their sadomasochism encompassed—this breast-pinching. At Château 19, the man had been shocked by what he saw and was forced to ask himself whether this was what he was really all about. He decided that it was not; but at the same time he found that he could not say as much for his girl friend. So he came to the conclusion that he was not a sadomasochist, that his girl friend was, and that he could not go with her any longer. This, if you will, is the truth which the man discovered at Château 19, and the consequences thereof.

The anecdote, Kosinski suggested to me, indicates what is happening to sadomasochism today at the hands of the modern market economy. Sadomasochism began as the authentic quest of a small core of people. Now, however, the experience has become institutionalized; S & M organizations, stores, magazines, nightclubs define what it is all about, and authentic needs are stifled or perverted as the individual no longer recognizes them and is forced into joining the great marching columns of our time.

It sounded pretty dreadful, I assured Kosinski, but I asked whether it really was necessary for the trucking executive to believe that the true nature of his breast-pinching frolics was to be discerned in the squalid debauchery (if that is what it was) of Château 19. Apparently, for little if any more reason than that both sets of activities go under the name of sadomasochism? What compulsion was the executive under to perceive *his* activity in terms of the very different activities of other people?

Kosinski answered that these things are not always a question of being logical; and I said that the deficiency to which he was pointing lay in the executive trucker, and not in "the system." I asked Kosinski to tell me, instead, about what bound *him* to sadomasochism.

The distinction implied in the term, he answered, is phony. "I don't believe there are sadists," he said. "That's a truly inauthentic fad. Man is basically a victim, not in the sadomasochistic way of inviting pain but because his existence ends painfully and because he is victimized by society, by disease, and by so many other traumas."

The real attraction of sadomasochism, he went on to explain, is that it offers the possibility of experiencing more and performing less. In his relationship to women, man acts as performer and donor. This role is particularly problematic—and wearisome—at a time such as ours when there are no more supermen, and heroes and conquerors fail. But it is also an inherently unattractive role, Kosinski argues, because it is essentially servile and constrained, despite appearances. After all, it is the sadist who, bound by the obligations of his role, is serving the masochist. He pays attention to him, caters to his needs, gives him feeling. And he does not really get back anything in return. "Enough of the macho!" Kosinski exclaimed. "It's a trap in which you are caught, and in which you cannot have any movement!"

This is, Kosinski agreed, man's reply to women's lib—"You get on top, dearie!" Its relevance to sadomasochism, however, seems dubious to me, since the impulse to lie back and be served can be gratified in a wide range of more gentle ways than by being whipped by a dominatrix or two.

We did not get around to exploring these matters further. Kosinski produced an album of color photographs he had taken of a middle-aged man sitting in a garden chair on a lawn. In some of the photographs the man looked gregarious, in others he looked sad. In one photograph he was lighting a cigarette. These photographs, Kosinski explained, were of Jacques Monod, the Nobel laureate in biology and director of France's famous Pasteur Institute, and they were taken during the last thirty minutes of his life before he died of anemia. The cigarette he was lighting was his last cigarette.

Monod need not have died, since machines now exist to pump blood into bodies attacked by the particular disease from which he was suffering. However, he did not want to be hooked up to a machine. Monod's basic scientific theory, which has profoundly influenced Kosinski, is that there is no plan in nature, and that destiny is written concurrently with each event in life rather than prior to it.

8/ Noise

SOME TIME AGO THE ROLLING STONES PUT OUT
an album of black music and the blues, and—yes, you
guessed it—they called it *Black and Blue*; and to make
sure the album was part of today and now and where
it's all at, they advertised it on a billboard which de-
picted a beautiful woman whose dress was brutally
ripped and whose lovely body was cruelly tied by ropes
that also held her hands stretched helplessly high
above her head.

And so that even the dumbest pleb would get the
message, she also had a big black-and-blue bruise on
one cheek.

The story goes that when Mick first saw the
model who had been chosen for this pose, he objected
that she was too beautiful. But it didn't take him long,
apparently, to see the absurdity of his argument, and

soon he was so deeply into the act that he couldn't help but participate in the laborious chore of binding her up and roughing her up *gratia artis.*

And then there's Kiss. These "furious, fire-breathing, blood-vomiting, stage-bombing, toilet-wrecking madmen," to quote a fan magazine (a fanzine), were recently identified by a Gallup poll as teen America's favorite rock group.

Imagine this: Julius Streicher and Albert Speer have pooled their resources and, working under the singularly intense inspiration of the occasion, are designing a pageant for Heinrich Himmler's birthday party.

Imagine that and you get some idea of what Kiss is like. Even Kiss's name would have fitted well into the festivities, by the way, since the group makes a point of printing the last two letters of the word with the same twin lightning bolts designed by *der treuer Heinrich* for *his* organization.

Kiss's gestalt would have been familiar and welcome to the SS leader. "Unencumbered by any semblance of restraint they personify human greed and lust—acknowledged and amplified—sanctioned and given expression for an entire generation, bizarre but glamorous, openly erotic, slickly packaged. Cosmic."

That's from a Kiss fanzine, not a paean in *Der Stürmer* to Himmler's Death's Head boys in black. And "Hotter than Hell," "Destroyer," and "Dressed to Kill" are not SS slogans to counterpoint the monotonous *Sieg Heil*s of Hitler's more prosaic followers, but titles of

Kiss albums—each of which has sold more than a million copies.

Seven-inch platform heels on knee-length boots are standard Kiss garb, and add to their inhuman appearance. Images of death, violence, and destruction, as well as satanic frolics, dominate their concerts.

The kids get into the act not only by attending Kiss's Nuremberg rally concerts and buying their souvenir dross in vast quantities, but also by wearing replicas of Kiss outfits on which, reports have it, they sometimes spend fabulous sums of money.

Particularly revolting, even among these pustules, is the dolt who calls himself Gene Simmons, but who was born Gene Klein in Queens, New York.

Klein's predilection is for sticking out his abnormally long, apelike tongue and vomiting fake blood on the stage. He also specializes in blowing great balls of fire from that same mouth, which, regrettably, has not yet been scorched by the act. The spikes of Klein's boots, we're told, were designed to symbolize impalement. His facial makeup is supposed to resemble a "famous, ancient Oriental woodcarving, which just happens to symbolize death." And the blood-dripping, body-impaling Dracula imagery is supplemented, in Klein's outfit, by S & M bondage chains stretched across his chest. These are sometimes linked by another chain that's attached to a collar around his neck.

Nowhere do our semieducated intellectuals (the kind who dig Pachelbel's Canon in D Major and say it's great for getting high on) find a more accommodating outlet for their pretensions to existential insight and social comment than in punk.

Punk is, in the words of the aptly named John Rockwell of *The New York Times,* "a symbol of the restless energies of a youthful subculture that found industrialized bourgeois society hypocritical, self-satisfied and stale." This critic discovers in punk a profoundly concerned idealism. He reports a concert given by an English group, the Sex Pistols, in Atlanta. The SPs were singing a song called "Pretty Vacant." After a few repeats of the refrain, "We're so pretty, oh so pretty VA-CANT," the crowd bellowed out the word "vacant" along with the singer, a young gentleman named Johnny Rotten, who capped it all by screaming, "AND WE DON'T CARE!"

Du holde Kunst! some cap, no? But according to Mr. Rockwell, who was there, "the irony was that he screamed it with such passion and terror—with such *caring*—that you realized instantly that he cared a whole lot." And Rockwell adds sagely, "The punk's nihilism has always implied its opposite, as any good dialectical Marxist might have guessed. . . . It's probably safe to say that the band's biggest fans, in this country especially, have been the most roseate optimists and idealists about the future prospects of mankind."

Well, well, well. Roseate optimists and idealists notwithstanding, it's difficult to be persuaded by this particular exercise in dialectical Marxism. (Are there other than dialectical Marxists, by the way?)

And then Mr. Rockwell goes on to say, "Not all Pistols fans want to overthrow the existing order, necessarily, but to infuse it with new life."

"Not all . . . necessarily."
We've heard this kind of logic before. In a sense,
it is nothing more than a perversion of the divine voice
which ordered Jeremiah the prophet "to root out and to
pull down, and to destroy, and to overthrow; to build
and to plant."

But these boys here are not into planting or building except as a rationalization for the meaner things
they sing about getting into. Things like: wanting to be
anarchy, to get pissed off, to destroy, to kill, to mention
just a few of the enthusiasms expressed in their songs.

Where's the infusing of new life in all this?
Where's the vision? Punk is not about making omelets,
it's about breaking eggs; as Arthur Tress would say,
there is no metaphysical position in it. Only intellectuals' gibberish can find in punk the opposite of what it
represents itself as being.

One of the great philosophers of the punk
movement is a fellow called Danny Fields, now the
manager of the Ramones, who are the most successful punk group in the United States today. Danny is
a Phi Beta Kappa from the University of Pennsyl-
vania ("a major in English and a minor in Brooks
Brothers"); he then went on to Harvard Law School,
from which he dropped out when he was twenty
years old.

For glimpses of what Phi Beta Kappa achievement at an Ivy League school can do for you, here's
Danny, "friend of Lou Reed and Andy Warhol," as he
is quoted in a recent *Village Voice* tribute.

> Death is one of the only things that can make you wonder. It's good show business. It's the longest running show of all time. It has a very high audience participation rate. . . . People live fast and die young, and a lot of beautiful corpses are left lying around. There was a time when people I knew were dying at the rate of one a month. They took too many drugs or whatever. But that doesn't make them any less fabulous. Anyway, most of my favorite people are dead. Martha Mitchell . . . Carmen Miranda . . . James Dean . . . I mean, think of it! Almost everyone fabulous is dead!

I mean yes, *do* think about that one. We're told everybody calls him "Danny," "the same way they always call Andy 'Andy,' " and that Mickey Ruskin, who's run some of the hippest night spots in town, calls Danny "one of the most important people in the world." Some tribute, no?

We're also told that Danny's greatest asset is his taste. He's wild about: heavy romanticism, Van Gogh, Miklos Rosza film scores, Joan Baez's voice in "Farewell Angelina." Danny's very big on fantasy, too, and on the macabre. That is to say, he's very big on (1) underground comics and (2) the 1940 version of *The Thief of Baghdad,* which he calls "the greatest work of art of the twentieth century."

No wonder that Mickey Ruskin compares Danny to Leo Castelli. I mean, like, Danny's similarity to one of the world's great art dealers is so obvious that you're amazed you never noticed it before.

One of the punk rituals you see quite often—is when the band or members thereof spit at the audience. And while the members of the audience are being saturated, they spit back at the stage or else throw empty beer cans at their heroes to express their admiration. This sort of behavior doesn't always occur, of course. A punk nonritual is that punk audiences never applaud, as regular people do. When a punk audience is really turned on, it simply sits and waits for the next number to be played. Which perhaps is not a bad way to express appreciation.

"We're not into pretty or smooth, man," a punk musician from Boston growls. "We're into life. Life is ugly. Life is mean."

A few dippings from the punk lexicon—names of bands, their singers and songs. Dead Boys. Hot Knives. Werewolves. Rat Scabies. Bitch. Crime. Stone Man. Blitzkrieg Bop. Aliens. Clash. Richard Hell. Stranglehold. Vultures. Kinks. Sic Fux. The Jerks. Malpractice. Kong-Ress. Black Holes of Space. Storm Troopin'. Blowjobs. Manic Panic. The Dictators. Killer. Rocket to Russia. Dead Commies. Search and Destroy. The Stilettos. I am Sick. Sniffin' Glue. Heart Full of Napalm. Kill Me. Madame of Madness. Mondo Bondage. Quay Lewd. The Dogs. Master Race Rock. Ron the Ripper. The Criminals. The Grenades. Death Race. Alan Suicide.

Here's Paul Hendrickson writing in the *National Observer* about the punk bands. "They sing about anarchy, alienation, violence, drugs, sex, teen rebellion

—in short, any and every lesion on the dark, ripe under-belly of American life. Their lyrics are rawer. But then so is society."

Something got lost in the translation, I guess, since we're not told what society and their lyrics are rawer than. But let's not cavil about that. Anyone who can tell us that sex is a lesion on the dark, ripe under-belly of American society certainly deserves a hear-ing.

Very macabre, some of these boys. Richard Nolan, lead singer in the Third Nail, is a free-lance embalmer. Forty-five dollars a body, if you've ever won-dered how much it could set you back; and for a mere fifteen Dick will arrange the flowers, too. Dave Vanium gave up his grave-digging job, when his group, the Damned, began getting more bookings. The Damned's drummer, by the way, has the engaging name of Rat Scabies. But back to Dave. He's the group's lead singer. Caroline Coon tells us he looks as if he were "immacu-lately arisen from Dracula's crypt. On stage, he hisses like an angry bat."

Caroline, by the way, is the author of a book about punk, which, for some inaccessible reason, is en-titled *1988*. Here she's talking about Johnny Rotten at the Punk Rock Festival. "He wears a bondage suit. It's a black affair [so what else is new?] dangling with zips, chains, safety pins and crucifixes. He is bound around the chest and knees, a confinement symbolizing the urban reality he sees around him."

The rot, though, is creeping on apace. Or that, at least, is what can be inferred from Caroline's description of the change that's been coming over Johnny lately. "Once he moved over the stage squirming and jiggering around like a spinderly, geigercounter needle measuring radio activity," she recalls. "Lately, he rarely moves. He can be quite sickeningly still. This deathly, morgue-like stance sets skins crawling, and his lyrics are as suffocating as the world they describe."

Talk of collecting exotica! Can you imagine knowing enough about Johnny Rotten to recognize that he's no longer the spinderly geigercounter he once was? Boggle! And think of suffocating while your skin is crawling. . . .

"I Wanna Be Me," Mr. Rotten sings.

Is he *really* having any difficulty on that score?

I received a complete set of *Punk* magazine, which has been publishing every other month since January 1975. It's going to be quite a collector's item, and, frankly, I can hardly wait to get rid of it. *Punk* is about as bad as you would expect something like that to be, but it's not without its own charm. The editors explain in the first issue: "We don't believe in love or any of that shit. We believe in making money and getting drunk." And by the fourteenth issue—that's the "War Issue—Death to the Enemy!"—at least the first part of this commitment finds expression in an ad for Sex Pistols T-shirts, on which the "X" of "sex" is a swastika. "This ad banned from *N. Y. Rocker* and *Rolling Stone!*" the ad proudly proclaims.

Recently, the people who bring you *Punk* magazine put out a "Punk Manifesto," which was printed in the *Village Voice* right next to illustrations from the comic-book version of *The Story of O.* Here are some extracts from it. "There is no rock and roll in Russia. There is no artistic freedom, there is no McDonald's. Punk started as an attitude that celebrated American culture and the teenager as the Master Race. It wasn't a sexual, faggot hippie blood-sucking ignorant scum as the media would have you believe." Then on to the media, with their "pantywaist liberal pleas for humanity": The media, *Punk*'s manifesto declares, are "responsible for more crimes than the CIA and the Nixon administration put together. The media has turned the country into a bunch of soft, guilt-ridden neurotics content with disco music, *People* magazine, and watching *Three's Company,* a TV show which is not very funny."

(Disco, let me point out, is a *Punk* magazine pet peeve, though of course that isn't a sentiment shared by all punks. *Punk* magazine is indefatigable in expressing its sentiments on this score. "Kill yourself. Jump off a fuckin' cliff. Drive nails into your head. Become a robot and join the staff at Disneyland. OD. Anything. Just don't listen to discoshit," the magazine advises. "I've seen that canned crap take real live people and turn them into dogs! And vice versa. The epitome of all that's wrong with Western civilization is disco. Eddjicate yourself. Get into it. Read *Punk!*" was how one message concluded. But back to the manifesto.)

Just because Joe McCarthy was a schmuck, just
. because Vietnam was an embarrassing fiasco brought on by incompetent leaders, just because the CIA makes mistakes, doesn't mean the Communist Threat is any less real. Start seeing Com-

munism for what it is—a threat to freedom, choice, self-determination, and the right to openly criticize those who control the system. Why do you think they put up the Berlin Wall? The Iron Curtain is still there, the media just thinks the Son of Sam is better copy this year. America is besieged on every side by critics. These critics would be called something else in Soviet Russia—they would be called "prisoners."

And then on:

Disco music is a Russian plot to make the country docile so these pinko bastards can march right in without firing a shot! Punk on the other hand wakes people up. It is a revolutionary action to listen to rock and roll in Communist countries. Blue jeans sell for $100 a pair. The Communist Party calls rock 'n roll "decadent"—they just don't know what a real party is! Celebrate that we live in the greatest country in the world! Be proud to be an American, listen to loud, blaring rock 'n roll, get drunk, and remember—you are *Alive.*

I went down to SoHo to speak with John Holstrom, the twenty-five-year-old editor of *Punk* magazine, to see what other surprises that might produce. John is a nice kid, although you would think he was seventeen rather than twenty-five, and he took me to a restaurant where I could buy him dinner and talk with him. Actually, the whole thing was quite boring, and although he is a nice kid, he didn't seem all that bright, though I guess one has to respect his fortitude in keeping the magazine going despite the fact that newsstands won't carry it and almost no one advertises in it.

"We just thought we had to make a stand," John said by way of explaining the manifesto. "If you don't, people really confuse you, you know." The waitress brought the Jell-O dessert before she brought the potatoes for the roast beef. So, all in all, it seemed that this was going to be an evening of non sequiturs and that there was nothing to be done about that but to let them all hang out. John revealed that the Ramones and the Dictators and the Dead Boys are all right-wingers and agree with the Punk Manifesto.

Some epigrams from our conversation which you might care to quote, with or without attribution to Mr. Holstrom: "Punk is to white what soul is to niggers." "The reason you start a rock group is to get laid. It's the best thing about rock." "Writing is to cause trouble, just to attack, you know. I mean, like, look at Voltaire, you know." "I don't understand sophistication. I understand comic books and crude TV shows."

John is big on attacking. "Going to bars, starting fights, smashing up cars, destroying windows—it's fun, just for the hell of it, to get people mad at you. There's no aim to it. It's not a calculated thing, it's just something you naturally do. Either you feel that way or you don't.

"I really like to cause trouble," he adds, perhaps a bit superfluously. But he goes on to say that there can be some purpose to all this, and he specifies the problems addressed in the manifesto. "Like, people are embracing communism all over America," he points out.

"And I really agree with Ayn Rand's stuff, you know, like the individual against the collective. The hippie thing was just a lot of bullshit, just communism and collectivism. I believe in me. I don't believe in collective stuff, you know. If there's an energy crisis going on, I want the biggest car in the world, you know, and I want a Learjet and a house in Greenwich, and all. That's what this society, like, stands for, and I like that. If these people want collectivism and communism they should go to Russia and work in the salt mines or pick grapes or whatever."

In addition to Ayn Rand, John also mentioned some comic-strip character, whose name isn't decipherable from the tape recording, as the other major source of intellectual inspiration for him.

But the main point about attacking things, John insisted, is that it is fun. Culture is full of violence, he remarked: Just look at Bugs Bunny. "To me," he went on to say, "violence is fun. It's everywhere, I mean, like you look at Shakespeare, *The Taming of the Shrew,* it's just blood and guts, it's entertainment, it's great, it's really funny. Aggression is a form of entertainment, not a way of achieving an end—that's the main thing to know, you know."

Over coffee, another epigram was forthcoming: "The rock 'n' roll guitar is like a gun." Indeed, John continued, "Rock 'n' roll is a form of war, a rock concert is like an assault, you know. What the kids want is World War III, and we're giving it to them. People like war. My buddy Legs McNiel started a group called Shrapnel, and the theme of the group is war, and they come out in uniform and all."

119

And then there's a lass called Nico, whose big hit is "Deutschland Über Alles." John didn't know what that meant until I told him, but he knew he loved the song. He can trust his instincts, it seems. Nico, according to John, is another big fan of war, and apparently her *bon mot* is that war is the most exciting of times, or something like that. "Some groups are against the government," John added. "Like MC5, who're from Detroit and walk around with swastikas and submachine guns. But whether they're against government or for it, you know, in one way or another they're all militaristic."

He mentioned that many punks join the Marines.

John does not know why people get so worked up when they see something like a swastika on an album sleeve. "It's all power, you know. Like S & M bracelets, the guitar and all, it's power. You get the audience under your control and you confuse people—keep 'em guessing so they don't know what's coming next. That's what Hitler did. It's like telling a good story, you know; you capture the audience's mind."

When the check came, John said earnestly, "There's no philosophy in all this, you know. You gotta remember that."

I said I didn't think that was something I was likely to forget.

I decided to check out Helen ("I love my knives") Wheels because she seemed like the punkperson it would be least unpleasant to talk to. At twenty-nine, she is older than most punksters, and combining that with the fact that she has a college degree (from the State University of New York's Old Westbury College, a lin-

gering relic of sixties hippie experimental education),
I thought it also probable that she would be more artic-
ulate and thoughtful than most others.

Helen, who's known around the rock scene for
the very tough people she hangs out with—Hell's Angels and all—has two goldens and one platinum to her
credit already. (Sales of five hundred thousand records
bring you the former; a million get you the platinum.)
She's definitely a very macabre lady in many ways, but
she's not without very real promise, either. Here's one
of her lyrics, copyright 1977 and reprinted by kind permission of Helenback (what else?) Music, Inc.:

> deep in the heart of Germany
> Lucy clutched her breast in fear
> she heard the beat of her lover's heart
> for weeks she raved, in dreams he appeared
> from far-off Transylvania.
>
> only a woman can break his spell
> pure in heart, who will offer herself
> to Nosferatu.
>
> the ship pulled in without a sound.
> the faithful captain long since cold.
> he'd kept his log to the bloody end—
> last entry read "rats in the hold,
> my crew is dead, I fear the plague."
>
> mortal terror reigned
> sickness now. then horrible death.
> only Lucy knew the truth
> and at her window . . . Nosferatu.

so chaste so calm she gave herself
to the pleasure of her dreaded master,
he sucked the precious drops of life
throughout the long and cold, dark night.

"one last goodbye"
he was blinded by love.
one last goodbye
he was blinded by love.
blinded by love.

he screamed with fear. he'd stayed too long in her
   room.
the spell was broken; with a kiss of doom
he vanished into dust
whispered, "I am gone"
(left her all alone)

only a woman can break his spell
pure in heart, who will offer herself
to Nosferatu.

I found Helen in the big, grungy, interesting loft
which she and her band use as a practice studio. A
short, very energetic-looking lady, her hair all frizzed
out and dyed orange, real mean-like, she nevertheless
had a poignant quality that made one feel protective
toward her, which was odd.

Particularly odd, in fact, because she had two
little knives dangling from her earlobes, a bit of bone
(human, as she later informed me) as a sort of brooch
on one shoulder, and a rather authentic-looking metal

badge dominated by a swastika on the other. One of her wrists was heavily tattooed, although it was difficult to make out the design. On the way into the loft, she pointed to a glass tank in which two very healthy-looking boa constrictors were at temporary rest. A cage containing some nice playful white mice was perched above them: the dinner getting its exercise, it would seem.

Helen had just received from her dentist a pair of fangs, made from dental false-tooth material, which she would be using in her act. She put them on to show me, real Nosferatu-like, and explained that she likes to run out into the audience and bite a few people's necks with the fangs. The people out there get all excited by this, it seems. And when she's had enough of that, she climbs over their tables on the way back to the stage, sometimes spilling their drinks, which gets them real mad.

"I identify a tremendous amount with the, like, animal part of myself," Helen confided. She likes wearing animal costumes and makeup and perfume and all, because, as she says, there's a lot of power in that. I asked her why she wants to bite people in the neck and, altogether, why she carries on in the way she does. She answered by reciting one of her lyrics, "Room to Rage," which is also quoted here by kind permission of the copyright holder, Helenback Music, Inc. (1977):

I been beat to hell. I never get no help
& I made it through this lousy mess all by myself
alone & filth. what it is to hate.
& I made it through this long long night
   though it hurt so bad . . .

throw the curtain wide & clear the stage
everybody you step aside & gimme room
I need room to rage

The power of her recitation was stunning and brought distant but nonetheless plausible evocations of Edith Piaf to mind. What is Helen's rage all about?

"The song is totally autobiographical," she said. "I was always overly psychic and was declared mentally ill and was totally chemically unbalanced and was treated as a total chemotherapy patient . . .

"But it was like choosing hell, too, and it was when I started writing songs that I started coming out of that and I realized I could heal myself. I always knew I was a brilliant writer, but I never wrote songs, and that, and then singing, was first the vehicle to save my life and then it became the vehicle for my art."

Specifically, I asked, what *was* the hell? "It was being mentally ill," she replied, "a totally downtrodden person in the East Village in an apartment full of rats. No money. Welfare. A brilliant artist who couldn't express herself. A person who was a poet but for ten years couldn't recite her stuff. Real tunnel vision. Paranoia. Fear. Stuff like that . . .

"But I don't live in hell anymore," she continued. "I feel, like, open, brave. No one fucks with me anymore because I've grasped my own integrity and I've taken control and responsibility for myself. The rage is still there, but it's not directed at *me* anymore. Now it's just something I'm expressing. I'm expressing my feelings of rage, but they're just feelings, they're not directed at anyone or anything.

"All my stuff's not anger," she hastened to add. "But in my act I do contact with a lot of that. I use a lot of violent props. I use blank pistols, knives—many of them are given to me by fans. They'll give me filed-down ice picks and stuff like that. Generally, I'll cut myself once because it stirs my histamines, and it's, like, very ritualistic, though I only do that in a small way nowadays . . ."

"You actually *cut* yourself?" I asked incredulously.

"Yeah," she replied in a matter-of-fact way. "Or sometimes I'll scratch myself deeply enough so that the knife leaves a deep-red mark."

"But doesn't it *hurt?*"

"No, not really. I've gotten quite injured on the stage, but you don't actually feel it till the next day."

"The audience loves that, does it?"

"It's real intense. I don't care if it's too intense for some people. I express my art quite openly and honestly."

She disappeared into her office for a moment and returned with a big black bag containing her props. And quite some props they proved to be as she spilled them out onto the floor. Cap pistols. Real switchblades. Knives and daggers of all sorts. Handcuffs. Chains. Thongs. A whip. Were these only stage props, I asked her—or were they something more than that?

"I love my knives," she answered. "And the guns are a symbol. I stick the gun in my pants like a cock, I use it for all the symbols it is. Life is pretty violent, you know. That's what I've observed in twenty-nine years." I asked her about the "jewelry" that adorned her. "It protects me from the outside world," she explained. "It shows I'm an individual, I got my own aura, and most people are really fucked up and don't use their brains very much.

"I like to wear black clothes," she added. "I like black leather, and very nasty, aggressive clothes. Also, they're important symbols of life to me, that is, the knives are. They're neat. A knife is a very important symbol. It's frightening. It's violent. It's phallic. It's lots of things and has a lot of effect on people. When I hold a knife in a performance, it's a very electric charge. I often cut myself with it, or I lick the knife or at a very dramatic moment in the music I'll smash it into the floor . . .

"It's like a magic, pagan act," she went on to say. "I take a tone of anger that could eat my heart out and make me hate myself and just—BAM!—put it into a piece of wood where it doesn't hurt anything or anybody. It's real powerful that way!"

"But what," I asked, "are you telling your audience? Is it just a matter of expressing how you feel, or are you speaking for them, do you think? Or perhaps telling them something they should know but don't?"

"It's like this," Helen replied. "I'm trying to tell these people something. I'm very moralistic, I'm very conscious of the moralistic thing in my songs. One thing I don't do—a lot of my dearest friends in bands like the Dead Boys and so on, they're real nihilistic, and they just come out and say 'Kill that girl, stab! stab! Fuck you, we hate you!' All that, which is not my trip at all.

"My publishing company is called Helenback because I've been there and I love life and I've seen a side that most people haven't seen, and I still choose to be there a lot, but my songs have a sort of lesson for people that, man, you have to destroy to create, you have to break down what's fucked up before you can start with a clean slate. It's an amazing joy to show people you can express yourself without killing yourself. I now can enact, portray, suicide, but when I do that, it's real and shows you don't have to actually do it. That's why punk is super-healthy, because people can see all these super-violent things and they don't have to go home and kill people or kill themselves. . . . Here in the States the kids have more money, perhaps more future, than in England, but they're still spiritually dead and they don't have the kinds of things we had in the sixties . . ."

Helen Wheels continued, "I have a great conscience about what I am saying to people. If I write a song about violence totally from the point of view of the person who committed the crime, I mean, he's left there hanging in jail for twenty-five years, and at the end of the song I'm handcuffed to the mike and I'm pulling the thing so hard that my wrist will start to get cut, and I will feel how it feels to be condemned by your own fucking stupidity to twenty-five years in jail: It will all show on my face, and I portray it to these people so they don't have to make that mistake, just like I don't have to. And yet, you see, I can experience it all without hurting anybody, without being hurt. So, you see, I know I got, like, soul; I got astral contact. I feel alive spiritually, and I've got something to tell these people who are so lost. That's what I do in my songs."

9/Christopher Makos: Trash 'n' Thrash

"CHRISTOPHER MAKOS IS THE MOST MODern photographer in America," says Andy Warhol.

You might think this is a bit like saying that someone's got a real nice personality when asked if she's good-looking, but when Andy says someone's very modern, it's a compliment of the highest order, and it means Chris is a real important photographer. It also means that Chris is a friend of Andy's, or, at least, that he's part of the menagerie the Campbell soup man has clustered around him in his factory on lower Broadway. In fact, lots of Chris's pictures of Andy and his pals and others appear in *Interview,* Andy's own magazine, if you ever look at that.

Chris's first book, *White Trash,* was published in 1977. It is an extraordinarily mean and menacing assemblage of photographs of the punk scene at all levels of society. Its appearance caused a sensation, which was eased along not a little by Chris's flair for delivering himself of such opinions as "All artists are fascists" and "Photography is an act of violence. The camera is a knife."

Makos's work has been compared, both in its intention and its achievement, to that of Hogarth, Daumier, and Goya, which, of course, shouldn't lead you to think he's any the less modern for that, and, besides, *High Times* says that having your picture taken by Chris is one of the last status symbols around. Chris is only thirty years old, and a very boyish thirty at that, but despite all the hype, he has already influenced contemporary photography to a striking degree, and it's probably true to say that he is one of the more important and interesting photographers around.

I went to visit him at his small tenement apartment in the Village. A few pieces of Salvation Army furniture, Mantovanilike music coming out of a little stereo, a Man Ray lithograph—affectionately inscribed to Chris—of Sade with the Bastille burning behind him, and lots more lithographs by Andy affectionately inscribed to Chris. Also on the walls: two super color photographs of the Concorde taken by Chris, who is entranced by the plane and wishes he had enough money to fly in it.

He said that his work has always been of the racy, fast, raunchy side of life. "That's so much of what New York is: fast, vulgar, obscene, all those things which make New York the great place it is." Has he ever photographed other kinds of things, did he per-

haps go through a lyrical period, or anything like that?"
I inquired.

"Like pretty pictures of flowers and scenes of lakes, and stuff?" he asks. "No, never. I'm very true in my work, I think. I hope I am. I just hate pictures of nature. I feel that that kind of stuff you should just go and experience. If you want to see a beautiful sunset, go look at it. I hate photographs of beautiful sunsets. Sometimes—it's not with everybody, but sometimes—if you have sex with people and you have a photograph of it, you have it forever. It's also because I forget so much. For me a photograph is a reminder that it's there. When I'm not with people, it's as if they barely exist for me. They do in my memory. . . . It seems complex, I guess. My mind works in a very weird way, I suppose."

"And what is that?" I asked.

"Well, I'm always staring at things. Always staring. I'm always amazed at people when I see them. They usually look blank when they're walking on the street, looking straight ahead of them. They don't see all the stuff that's going on. And that, for me—looking at everything all the time and staring at everything, which is what I do—that really takes its toll, because all that input and information coming into my mind can really knock you out. If I don't have a way to get out of that, like through magazines or doing books or telling stories to people, I would go really crazy."

"But why does the violence and squalor of punk come out, when there is so much else that's also flowing into you from the environment? What makes that particularly important, or fascinating?"

"I'm much more fascinated with that," he replied, "because I don't see that all the time. The sun I've seen every day since I was born. All the stuff that's coming out now, because of my religious background, I guess, is stuff that really fascinates me. I come from a very strict Catholic background—I hate to sound like one of those Catholics who is driven by guilt—but the seedy side of life *does* fascinate me, because it also appears to be the highest side of life. It's like going around with Andy Warhol and seeing the society people. They have their own squalor. The middle class is the cleanest, most clean-cut. The very poor and the very rich people are the ones who live in squalor, either emotional or real."

"But what makes squalor more real than the setting sun," I persisted. "Why is it the highest side of life?"

"There are many more things to look at in squalor than in the clean-cut life," he explained. "I get so insecure when I travel to the Midwest or even L.A., where everything is so clean and looks like there are no problems. I like it just for short periods of time, but it does not make me feel like I'm alive. Nothing comes out at me. It has a very numbing effect on me, and I like to feel I'm alive. I like to have things poking at me, and making me feel, like, Christopher, wake up, you're alive!"

"Is that why you're involved with violence?"

"The seventies is a period of great physical violence, but also of emotional violence—there's so much of that around. I need constant probing by my friends and people and lovers to tell me that life is real interesting and that there is no need to chuck it all away, and that it is worth living."

"But why Sade and the Bastille? There are many other aspects to life, are there not, which could make you feel alive?"

"There are millions. There's baseball, football, soccer, and all the things . . . you just don't have time for them."

"But why have you gone in this particular direction?"

"Because it keeps me awake. I'm just always in a zombie state, it's hard for me to keep awake because I'm numbed by the TV and the magazines and everything else. It hypnotizes me. I find myself reading *People* magazine and wasting time reading shit like that. Wasting time watching some TV show that draws me in. It's, like, my way of escaping from all that input and information coming at me from all around, but it's just as hypnotizing in its own way, which is actually much worse than the effect of real life. So between the real world and that crap I find myself like a zombie. Sometimes I let myself be beaten. I don't really like that, but it wakes me out of a zombie state. . . . I don't really like it, because it hurts; but that's not actually the main thing, because sometimes it goes beyond that and then I realize I'm awake and that's fine . . . ."

"So it's the hurting that you don't like, but it's the being awake that you do like, and for you it is the way of being awake, of freeing yourself from the hypnotic effects of *People* magazine, which itself is a way of escaping the hypnotic effects of living in a hyper-stimulating world? Is that it?"

"I suppose that must sound unusual, but, yeah, that's about it. A friend and I slap each other in the face, and it's just great."

"And how does punk fit into this? White trash?"

"Punk is anarchy against the self, really. Look at the way they dress. It says so much when you look at that: They're screaming, 'Hey, look at me, look at me, look at me!' They're just screaming all the time to get noticed in this big massive TV system of a world we live in. I think in the end some of them will just kill themselves and mutilate their cocks and faces or whatever to get attention. It seems like the only way. Like that author who jumped off the Brooklyn Bridge so that publishers would notice him and publish his book. It's easy to get lost in this world. I feel there must be some alternative before they take that big step—you know, the big one—to get attention. Sometimes I look out at the world and see how stupid people are, and how blind they are, and then I realize there's not much hope for them. The author who jumped off the bridge, and the man who was determined to go to the electric chair—Gilmore—and all those people: Is that what we're coming to? And that's why I just pay attention to myself, and realize that if I'm going to practice any violence or whatever, why let them do it to me—I might as well just do it to myself. But I'm not drawn to the punk scene myself any longer. It fascinated me for a short period. I liked the fashion element of it, and how people reacted to each other. It was like a small brush war inside the culture."

"Why did you move beyond it?"

"Because I'm always searching for new things and new people to keep me awake, and for me to keep them awake. I like a constant dialectic with society or my friends."

"You say," I mentioned, quoting from another interview, " 'I try to forget everything, not to have any memory. This is the price I pay for waking up new every morning.' Can you really expect to experience things in an authentic way when you wake up new every morning?"

"Oh, sure, it's just like a baby when it first experiences things. Of course, you can get burned if you do things this way. But being that I don't mind getting burned at all, the pain that life has, I really do try to do that. If you have a lover—you know how that love can be lulled away, that wonderful rush when you first fall in love, that great feeling every day: Life can just lull it away. I treasure these feelings of love and emotion that we are capable of, I try to hold on to them very much. But if I just keep remembering what they are like, I find myself being hypnotized back into that lull again. If I can try and forget the day before, each day is new to me. It's terrific that way! But I hold myself back from things that might be fun because I think I have so much of life ahead of me still that I don't want to blow myself with all these things to do."

"Does that sound as if you're anxious about depleting the stock of things to do?"

"Yeah, it's possible, I think. But I think it's very true to the nature of the universe to not remember. Intuitively, I don't just sit around and think about this at all. I just experience my life as it goes along every day."

"Isn't that lull, as you call it, part of experience,

though? Love cannot always be thrilling and new. Doesn't commitment extend beyond that? Or isn't commitment important?"

"I'm going through a very unusual period of my life now, which is that I *am* in love. It's true, I am going into this relationship, and it seems that parts of it can become numbing, so I am having to learn how to deal with this numbing effect. Because I also believe this other thing about experiencing fresh new images all the time, and it doesn't seem like love and this other thing go together very well. Because, I agree, love *is* commitment. I am sort of in conflict with myself about how I feel about that. But I feel it is really important to make commitments to things and objects and people, but I also think it's important to have this constant flux. There must be a good balance between the two. That's what I'm trying to learn right now. It's so exciting to experience so many people in one's lifetime, though, even if it is only for a short period of time. Even if it's just a short relationship, you can still learn a lot about each other, and also give a lot to each other."

"What are you giving someone through violence?"

"It's what they are giving me, too."

"And what are they giving you?"

"They are giving me, sharing with me, their experience that this is the way they feel, that they are unhappy and tormented in certain aspects of their lives. 'Christopher, look at this for a short period of time and see if you are unhappy, too, and if you are tortured by the same things I am.' But it also helps keep me awake, and that I can't explain, it's just something that happens."

"Does your work necessarily have to reflect this —this need to keep awake?"

"It's not only that. Right now I think I'm reflecting what is going on in America; there's really tremendous violence here. Last night I saw *The Fury,* a Kirk Douglas movie that was very violent. I saw *Carrie* just the other day, and that's about violence, too. And I guess that as an artist I reflect what is going on. I am like a sponge. I soak all this up as it comes and I throw it back to whoever wants to see it."

"Isn't there some hype in this, though? How much violence, really, is there in our society, as distinct from the fad that surrounds it? Are you into violence because everyone else is?"

"I don't think I am into it at all because of everybody else. I have always been exactly the way I am, and some people view that as being violent and not at all the norm. But I haven't changed my way of life at all because of what I think is a way to be, because of what other people make into a fad."

"But you called yourself a sponge. You say that you haven't been affected by the times, which is intrinsically improbable, because we all are in one way or another. And if you are a sponge, that *really* soaks things up, doesn't it?"

"But a sponge always resumes its original shape!"

"Assuming it dries out completely, which it may not. What is the original shape of this sponge?"

TERRORIST CHIC

"The shape of a timid boy from Massachusetts who really likes life in the fast lane—I hate the phrase, but it's true. I love New York, I feed on all this nutty activity people seem to be involved in. Sometimes I go through a period of wanting to party my way through life. Because you get so many quick experiences there, again—that chitchatting with people about nothing, people you may never meet again. You get to pass information like an underground railroad, you pass information about life to each other, your own life and their life . . ."

"What kind of information?"

"Things like what are they doing in life and how are they dealing with it all, whether they live alone, or whatever . . ."

"Isn't that pretty trivial information, though?"

"It *is* meager, but it acts as a foundation to all the big things in life: Nothing can be ignored in life—nothing. Meager, maybe; yeah. But it's like President Carter, his campaigning on a grass-roots level, that's where it was when he started out campaigning. We can't say that everything's just this big thing or else I'm not interested in it: We have to deal with all the little bits. But it's also as if I have all these personalities which the timid boy from Massachusetts sort of holds together. There was a show on TV called *Sybil,* where this girl has thirty-nine personalities or however many, and I said, God, so what? I have so many different sides, so many different facets to myself, that are not as clearcut and defined as that poor girl."

"There is a great danger, though, isn't there, in getting caught up with whatever is on the scene at the

138

moment—a danger of losing yourself?"

"There is a danger, but I think it's better to take a chance than not to take a chance at all. There is a danger in this sort of behavior, but I'm of the belief that it's best to take risks rather than let this thing pass by —whatever the thing at the time may be."

"But shouldn't everyone be set in their ways up to a point—with their own values, for example, and beliefs, which give them their own identity and continuity?" I asked.

"But you shouldn't inflict your values on other people," he replied.

"Sometimes you should. But my point is whether it's desirable not to have them—values, and so on, that one sticks by because they are the core of one's personality."

"I'm open to everything, but then I guess when it comes to deciding about things I'm not. Then I'm open only to what I want to do, and usually I know pretty much what I want in any situation."

"Is that consistent with being born again every day, though—this knowing what you want?"

"Yes, because you can decide that every day."

"Is there continuity reflected in that? Your real self, if you will?"

"That's hard, isn't it? You got me there. It seems like a very serious point. It is a little bit at odds, yeah ... But, you know, I do set a course, and you can go off it a little, but it is there; and when you cross the sea there are a lot of things that could happen, you know. You could see other ships, and icebergs and planes ... there are all those options out there and you check them out. But you know the course from New York to London, if you've decided on that course, and in my case I know I'm going toward death, or rather dying, and all these things are available and I shouldn't ignore them but should pay attention to everything and ignore nothing. And I should pay most of the attention to myself!"

"I suppose I'm talking about experiencing things from the basis of one's own identity and values, and I rather wonder whether a 'born again every day' person has such a basis beyond the mere lust for sensation."

"My value system is just that I don't like to see people killing each other or hurting each other, but up to that point I feel that everything is acceptable. If people want to pee on each other or shit on each other or scuff each other's shoes or slap each other in the face I think that's all fine. I just think that so many things are acceptable . . ."

"Particularly if they are new?"

"Yeah, but I do draw the line on murder and things like that, even if in some future society that may not be illegal if they have no more food and they have to kill each other to eat. But until that point arrives, I'm not in favor of things like that."

"What direction do you think your work may take in the next few years?"

"I'm trying to simplify it visually. I just want to see very simple images—just one leg, maybe two legs: but not the whole body. I'm into this close-up of things, staring at things, a sort of hypnosis between myself and my subject."

"Are you moving away from those images of violence and squalor and brutality?"

"I think I am. All my new photographs are pictures of people just experiencing life, parties, love, experiencing a drink, experiencing a whole lot of things. I think they might be brutal still, because many of them are done with a flash and real quick—no time to think."

"Is there room for beauty, and joy, in these?"

"I hope so. Also, through pictures of squalor, brutality, and so on, I hope that maybe it gives people hope that there's something more than this. You know, often it does give *me* that hope, that there are different levels of existence that are really enjoyable for long periods of time."

"But it's no more than an accident, you say, that you were into scenes of squalor at the time when lots of other people were?"

"Well, it's just that I live in a sort of central core of artists and other people who all seem to experience the same thing, to have the same experiences at the same time."

"How do you suppose a new thing like that gets started?"

"It's triggered off at these parties, you know, when people see the way the others dress. I think a lot of it happens with the way people dress, and people start judging books by their covers and begin thinking, 'Aha! this is the way things are supposed to be!' And then maybe they read a little tiny article somewhere in some magazine, and an artist will pick up on that . . . Things snowball in that way."

"Is that how it happened to you?"

"No. It didn't happen to me. I've just always been sort of into looking out for these new experiences, and it seems like a lot of new experiences are thrusting their way at me."

"But this then *did* become the new experience for you, three or four years ago?"

"Yeah."

"What's the new experience now that's behind the new kinds of photographs you're taking?"

"My new experience is that I realize that people pose a lot for my pictures, so now I don't aim my camera, I just hold it up and quickly do it, because if they're posing for me I'm going to be posing for them, too, and I want to try to get the most candid photo possible. I don't even look through the camera now, and I have reams of photos that all come out perfectly, really, with great cropping . . . I'll just get to see this person's eye, or whatever, and I think you really get to see a lot of a person by seeing those elements of them."

"But what started this off? You talked just now about how things get started as a result of what you experience at parties, and so on."

"People are really into seeing themselves now, buying these Betamax systems so that they and their wives or whatever can watch themselves fuck and then play it back. And they buy Polaroids so that they can photograph each other having sex and stuff, and see that immediately. People don't believe that they're experiencing what they're experiencing, it seems, so they have to have these machines to show it back to them: 'This is really happening, wow, this is really happening

—here's a picture to prove it!' Technology has allowed us to see this really fast, and I'm just taking it one step further, which involves holding up my little camera and letting it snap away."

"So that's the wider setting of your new work?"

"Yeah. I think there's going to be quieter moments ahead for all of us, but right now this is what I seem to be photographing, and even when I'm photographing beautiful scenes, a beautiful woman, or whatever, or a terrific party, this whole idea of snapping them up real fast seems to be a sort of violent way of doing it, rather than a very lush setting up of the photograph like Arthur Irving Penn and the people in the forties and fifties were doing. I guess it's a desperate attempt at realizing that you have to get what you have to get *now,* that there's no point in wasting time, because movies and TV have made us able to look at ourselves. I often wonder what people like Lucille Ball feel like, how they can just turn on a TV set and see their images from twenty or forty years ago, and here they are facing death now. What is that like to watch a whole period of your lifetime just disappear? This is probably the first period of history when people can see their whole lives on film. And how they deal with this and face death is a real problem. You can see your whole life flash by now without even experiencing death, so it's like even death is becoming pointless now, there's no retrospect to it all any longer. And that's why you have to get it all *now . . .*"

10/CBGB: Armpit of the Punk Scene

I'M STANDING IN FRONT OF CBGB AND FEELING pretty jeepy-creepy. Scared, that is. Not because of the bums wandering all over the Bowery or the traffic trying to steer clear of them and the potholes on the dimly lit street, but because I'm at the very armpit of the punk scene. Why scared? Well, if you're not scared at the thought of going into the den where safety pins through the earlobes and razor blades dangling from the neck and swastikas dripping blood-red paint are the order of the day, then you don't know what scared is. Here's where, according to columnists' reports, "infected human energy bubbling and growing beneath the surface, swelling with unavoidable and incandescent pus" finally hits the surface. Here's where the mottoes are "Look mean, dress nuts, talk bad, get your kicks off S & M, fuck over the suckers, jerk off the jerk-offs, life's a pretty mean party anyhow, do it before it does you, ha-ha, suicide'll get ya yet!"

Still not scared? Well, here's where a lady singer says the guitar's the new weapon, but if you don't have the bucks to buy strings, carry a knife. The folks here, I've heard tell, are nasty as spit. Boozed up or spaced out. Lookin' mean, talking dirty, pissed off, and fucked over. "You can look like a shit, but you don't smell like a shit unless you are a shit. Blood and guts are hot. Death's the ultimate orgasm. Murder makes you come. Fucking and killing are the same. Get off on gore."

I hesitated under the bulbous yellow canopy with CBGB and OM FUG written on it: Dante's gateway to hell —*lasciate ogni speranza*... A youth emerged from the door. He was wearing a thermal undershirt that was still recognizable as having once been white. "Destroy!" was written in big, crudely lettered red on the shirt. And above it there was a large swastika.

Apart from this, though, he seemed a nice enough fellow; the swastika was painted the wrong way round (it faced left), and he said goodbye to the bouncer at the door in a friendly, open kind of way.

The bouncer would have no trouble qualifying for the job at a nightclub for construction workers and truck drivers. He was wearing jeans and a denim shirt, and had long gray hair hanging down from underneath his bright-yellow helmet. He was a giant. But not a brute. In fact, his face actually had a kindly, if slightly bored, look to it. He pushed the door open with his pinkie to let me pass.

Inside, it was a long, black corridor, and four bucks before you could step more than a couple of feet from the door. I paid without really noticing it, though, because I was already feeling spaced out and pissed off and sensing lots of incandescent pus because the noise was so stupendous. It was a big Saturday-night crowd, and I had to push my way through to get something of a glimpse of the shabbily lit platform at the end from where the noise was coming. But people were very genial about letting me pass. One or two even said "Excuse me" as I barged by them, and I remembered to watch my manners.

There was a nagging sense of *déjà vu* that I couldn't quite pin down. The tidal waves of sound crystallized just a little, though, and—*snap!*—suddenly I got it.

It was the tune the band had been belting out. Was it a Perry Como number, or something from ol' Blue Eyes himself? I couldn't remember, but I hummed along all the same: "I've been a puppet, a pauper, a poet, a something, a pawn, and a king," or however it went. The song came to an end before I could recall more of the words—certainly the singers were doing little to help me remember them. Now there was a new number. A fellow who's lonesome despite the megawattage being amplified by his friends—or perhaps because of it—is singing something like, "I wanna girl friend, I wanna raise a family." CBGB-PQR, is this gonna be a bore?

I stopped at the bar. "WATCH OUT! PUNK IS HERE!" a sign said. I missed the one that said the smallest little bottle of Miller's I'd ever seen was going to set me back a buck and a half. But I did remember the nice man in the yellow hat and obligingly did not ask for a glass to go with the bottle, and could I have my beer at something colder than room temperature, please?

A tingle of—unpleasant—anticipation. A skinny, ugly-looking fellow squeezed next to me at the bar. There's no safety pin or razor blade on this dude, but the meaning of his long ginger-colored crew cut, gaunt face, pallid, spotty complexion is unmistakable: He's a real punk, the meanies and all. In case the message was not clear, he had a big button on his lapel that said, "FUCK YOU!"

Startled by this presence at my elbow, I dropped my matchbox on the floor. Before I had a chance to retrieve it, the FUCK YOU! kid had done so instead. He handed it to me with a polite smile, and after saying "Have a nice evening!," moved off into the crowd.

The crowd. They were an ugly-looking bunch for the most part, but more because nature intended things that way than as a result of any assist from the people concerned. There were more than the usual number of black clothes, but nothing really very kinky beyond that. A few girls wore sunglasses, very dark-colored ones with light frames. They would take these off every few moments because the place was so dark anyway that it would have been self-defeating not to. The clientele here tended to be in small groups and to stay very much with their own friends. There didn't seem to be very much of a pickup scene going on here. Nor, of course, very much of a punk scene, either. Most of the folks here looked pretty much as they probably do when they're at home watching the football game on TV.

Closer to the stage, there was a little more action.

Old Yellow Helmet pushed his way past to some kind of commotion ahead. A fight, evidently, but no real problem, since a few minutes later he headed back to his post at the door, still slightly bored and kindly looking, and with no over-boisterous punk dangling from his pinkie.

Someone had puked on the floor. It was already getting a bit crusty, and that's part of the scene, to be sure; but one couldn't help a lingering suspicion that none of the staff here wanted to get their hands on this particular piece of "infected human energy" that had surfaced. Over there, the FUCK YOU! kid had found a pal, who was rather more into the high-fashion bit than he: black leather jeans and jacket, plus short black leather gloves with heavy zippers running along their backs. Quite becoming, actually.

Pushing her way out—angrily, as though she had just been goosed—a heavy-duty lady went by. She had lightning flashes mascaraed on her cheeks and was wearing a black (cloth) jacket that was unbuttoned almost to the waist to reveal a beige underwire bra that even Anita Bryant might consider a bit prissy.

Over by the bar again there was a *very* punky-looking lady. No safety pins or razors or sunglasses, to be sure, but her short hair was all frizzed out to make it look real mean, and she had a lot of hard, cold makeup that made her look almost like Count Drac's sister. I couldn't help but wonder what *her* thing is likely to be behind closed doors, all the more so when I noticed the very Germanic-looking young blond man who was with her. His apparel was very straight, which only made hers look all the more far-out.

Far-out? She turned her head away when she sensed I'd been looking at her. And again I had that feeling of *déjà vu* . . .

Oh no! I recognized the lady: I knew her! She was a specialist in Marxist epistemology who was thrown out of the philosophy department of a minor university because she didn't finish her Ph.D. This lady—I'd had endless hours of debate with her defending myself against the True Believer's analysis of capitalism and the Vietnam war!

And here she was now: the punkiest woman around, and that, for sure, showed real epistemological cool. Just to check, though, I stopped to say hello, and it turned out that she was not, after all, doing a book on the scene but only hanging out and showing Fritzie or whatever his name was the New York scene. "Things are a bit quiet here tonight," she said, and looked bored.

Near the entrance, someone was tacking up a record sleeve of a group called the Suicide Commandos. Yellow Helmet gave me a nice smile and said goodbye, come again.

11/Terrorist Thrillers

THE BASIC THEME, OF COURSE, IS OF AN evil man or group—usually he or they are also brilliant and incredibly rich—who plot to hold the entire world to ransom. Or to enslave it. Or to destroy it.

This is not a theme cultivated specially for the paperback wilderness. In fact, it goes back almost a century. Sherlock Holmes, after all, had Dr. Moriarty to contend with; and after the two of them were out of the way, the Yellow Peril surfaced in the person of Dr. Fu Manchu. Thereafter, Dr. No and Specter and others came along to give James Bond much trouble.

When the hippies appeared in the sixties, threatening to destroy Agatha Christie's world of cucumber sandwiches and croquet on the vicarage lawn, that lady could explain matters only in terms of some unknown underworld Napoleon who was controlling the long-haired freaks for his own sinister purposes. "There are forces always at work," she wrote darkly in *Passenger to Frankfurt.* "But behind each of them there is someone who controls it."

But she, as well as Conan Doyle, Sax Rohmer, Ian Fleming, and others were all writing dressed-up versions of the old morality tale, which is the story of Pilgrim and his battles for law, order, civilization, and virtue. James Bond, admittedly, was no example of prissy propriety. But there is no doubt in your mind that, when he wins, all the good things in life are the beneficiaries.

The villains in these tales were kept obscure. As such, they served as almost blank screens onto which the reader could project his wildest imaginings. This, no less than curiosity as to how the villain would be foiled, helped counter the reader's foreknowledge—potentially anticlimactic as it is—that the villain would, in fact, be foiled. Another characteristic of these novels is that the story unfolds from the perspective of the hero, who is, indeed, an admirable character with whom the reader is tacitly encouraged to identify.

All this has changed in today's terrorist thrillers. Most obviously, in the revised version of the genre, the villains have emerged from their earlier obscurity and are often given at least as much coverage as their opponents. We do not look over the shoulders of Pilgrim alone, but over those of the Bad One as well, and as often as not we get to know each of them equally well.

This equal-time provision intentionally obscures the distinction between the two. The question the reader now faces, moreover, is no longer *how* the villain will be foiled but *whether* he will be foiled.

That is by no means a foregone conclusion any longer. In *The Trinity Implosion,* coauthored by Robin Moore (of *The Green Berets, The French Connection,* and so on), four men set out to build a nuclear bomb. And they succeed. And they detonate it. And: "One of the dual detonators in lens 34 failed to fire, but its companion did. AND . . . "

"Alexander, Tom and Hamid, and the pilot, marveled at the monster that had been unleashed. AND . . . "

"Millions of Americans were puzzled when the television image of the president of the United States suddenly turned black and nothing appeared on the screen for more than five minutes. The truth that would come within a half hour would spread panic throughout the land. AND . . . "

And—that's the way the novel ends. And so there is no question but that the bad guys don't always finish last anymore.

The villain is no longer a shadowy, unknown figure capable—precisely because of his obscurity—of stimulating the reader's fantasies. To compensate for the loss of tension this could cause, "realism" is now considered an essential ingredient in the new wave of terrorist thrillers. Instead of imagining *who* the villain is, we are locked into the story by massively detailed descriptions of machinery and settings and plans—which are almost always presented in terms of the villain's machinations. ("The box had a metal parts number plate on it that identified it as S.F.N.E.A. #CD-3625-21, which it was not." Actually, of course, it's a remote-controlled bomb planted in the tail assembly of an El Al Concorde.)

This "realism" is not just designed to make the implausible seem convincing, but to draw the reader into the plot until he becomes scmething close to a co-conspirator of the terrorists themselves. They—or certainly their plans—become so real and compelling that you can't help sort of hoping that they will succeed.

The most fundamental change in the new generation of terrorist thrillers lies in their depiction of what were earlier the heroes and the villains. This change occurs in either or both of two ways. One is to show that the villains are not really all *that* bad, or to suggest that they can't help doing whatever it is that they are trying to do. In *Black Sunday,* a best seller that sold over a million copies in paperback and was made into a successful movie, the terrorists hijack the Goodyear blimp and plan to explode it, and tens of thousands of steel darts, just above a crowded Super Bowl football game attended by the president of the United States. The perpetrators of this prank are a former U.S. navy pilot and an Arab woman. The pilot had been shot down over North Vietnam during the war and held prisoner in a cage for several years. Back home in the United States, he is being given a hard time by the bureaucrats of the Veterans Administration.

As for the Arab woman: Her troubles go all the way back to early childhood, when the Palestinian refugee camp in which she lived was bombed by the Israelis. In the movie version, she is played by the very beautiful Marthe Keller, whom we see almost at the outset of the film displaying her most attractive features in a shower.

So we get to know the terrorists. We get to feel familiar with them. And we get to feel some sympathy for them. The other side of the coin, of course, is that the good guys really aren't all that good. In *By the Rivers of Babylon* you just have no way of knowing who the hero is supposed to be. The terrorist leader is a psychopathic villain who digs his teeth into captured Israeli women and, besides, has been altogether too familiar with his own sister. You have no reason to like him. The El Al security chief who is his foremost adversary, however, is not really much more attractive than he. An Israeli lady aptly calls him "a Nazi," and you are not much sorrier when he gets killed than you are when the terrorist leader does.

In *The Tripoli Documents,* any doubts about the pot being blacker than the kettle are set to rest by the ruminations of an Arab terrorist and his Israeli adversary. First the Arab:

> Not murder. A death. All deaths are not murders. He was not a murderer. He was a fighter. He was a fighter for freedom, a freedom fighter. He was a soldier in the ranks. He was a fighter for a cause.
>
> A dirty word, terrorism. But not dirty when viewed within the full panoply of perspective. Terrorism is not mindless nihilism; it is a device, a tool of the weak, the enslaved, the deprived in their struggle against oppression.

> The tall man was flying toward a massive act of terror, but he felt no pang of conscience. He was a fighter, a fighter for a people, a freedom fighter, a patriot in a just cause.

Then the Israeli:

> Not a murder. A death. All deaths are not murders. He was not a murderer. He was a fighter. He was a fighter for freedom, a freedom fighter. He was a soldier in the ranks. He was a fighter for a cause.
>
> . . . he was flying toward a filthy little act of terror; it disgusted him, it was not his way, but in this world battles are fought on strange terrain, and he was a soldier in this struggle, a fighter for a people, a freedom fighter, a patriot in a just cause.

So—the tall Arab is going to commit a massive act of terror and feels no pangs of conscience, while the Israeli is going to commit only a little act of terror and is disgusted by it. But these fine distinctions aside, there really is not much to choose between the two men, and that, of course, is most studiedly the point. This does not mean that the reader puts a curse on both their houses, however. Instead, he joins in with each of them as though he were playing a game of chess against himself. That way, no one loses.

The first copies of Nelson de Mille's new terrorist thriller, *By the Rivers of Babylon,* were still being distributed to the booksellers when I called on him at his modest suburban house in Garden City, Long Island. A gleaming Cadillac Seville stood proudly in the driveway, an indulgence de Mille had allowed himself from the ample advances guaranteed by the Book-of-the-Month Club, which had taken the novel as a full selection, and Reader's Digest, which had bought it as a Condensed Book. Life had been good to de Mille this year, what with his first best seller and his first child, and he seemed quite charmingly dazed by the bounties that had befallen him.

An infantry officer during the Vietnamese war, de Mille is still a young man, but his hair is beginning to gray, and he worries about taxes. "Perhaps I'll move to Ireland," he said, "or maybe to England."

By the Rivers of Babylon is a smash thriller, I should say at the outset. The plot has two El Al Concordes filled with Israeli delegates flying to New York for a peace conference. The planes are hijacked by Arab terrorists, who actually blow up one of them in midair to show the pilot of the other that they mean business. (The destruction of the Concorde is one of the most spectacular events in terrorist fiction.)

The surviving plane is made to fly under radar level to a forced landing on the ruins of Babylon, in modern Iraq. While all the world is searching for the missing plane, the passengers refuse to surrender to the Arabs. Instead, they dig themselves in on a hilltop and fend off their assailants while waiting to be found and rescued. In this Middle Eastern version of *Lord of the Flies,* the defenders realize that they can survive only by abandoning the civilized restraints and ideals which they were carrying with them to the peace conference in New York. They proceed to do this with varying degrees of introspection and guilt. The novel is fast-paced, professional (de Mille is the author of a series of police thrillers), and maintains a frenetic tension until the very last page. While it is not "the greatest siege novel ever" described in a publicity handout, it is a compelling story and is told with a degree of political and psychological insight unusual for the genre.

De Mille, in our conversation, made a point of emphasizing that he is not particularly fascinated by terrorism or terrorists. "People pay an inordinate amount of attention to even the most trivial terrorist activities," he remarked. "Terrorism has become front-page news, but if you think about it for a moment, you realize that it is really not very important in the history of Western civilization. Terrorist objectives are short-sighted, and they wouldn't amount to much in a world situation even if the terrorists accomplished them— which they seldom do. If, indeed, they ever do."

I agreed with him and asked him why, in that case, he had decided to write a terrorist thriller in the first place. Well, he said, he was not even interested in terrorism and there are much larger world events that should be handled in novel form; yet his next novel is going to be about terrorists—this time, the IRA.

When one writer talks this way to another, it's a bit like two cabdrivers talking about the third center sprocket, left, inside their meters. It is insiders' talk, in other words, and it means that the writer is in thrall to publishing companies, and their editors, and their marketing mavens, and their sales directors, and their publicity experts, and all the rest of that great assemblage of consumer wizardry and literary discernment that stands behind many a writer's shoulder and inspires each tap of his fingers on the typewriter keyboard.

De Mille confirmed this diagnosis. "It was a publisher's idea," he said of the book. Bernard Geis had suggested the theme, "based on the headlines," and laid out certain specifics. For instance, that the book should be set sometime in the near future, that it should be an Arab-Israeli story, and that it should involve the hijacking of an Israeli delegation on its way to a peace conference. Moreover, de Mille continued, Geis suggested that the peace delegates should not surrender to their hijackers but should fight them off in some kind of siege situation.

Two reasons, he continued, pointed to the idea of the Israelis being peace delegates. One was to place them in a setting in which the feasibility of pacifism— or at least of peacefulness—is challenged by the demands of political actuality. The peace delegates must either fight or be killed; and if they are to fight, they must, because they are outgunned and outmanned, fight with a degree of ruthlessness which is entirely alien to their values.

The other reason for making the Israelis peace delegates is more intriguing, at least for our purposes here. Terrorism, de Mille had said, is "really not very important." Terrorist incidents, moreover, never really amount to anything much in terms of objective political considerations. Most terrorist attacks have been made on people who just happen to be around—schoolchildren riding on a particular train, or whatever—and even when victims are killed, the world is not significantly different as a result. To focus merely on the handful of human lives at stake in a terrorist incident, de Mille explained, is therefore not good enough for editors and publishers. *"You have got to have bigger consequences!"* he told me.

So if you want to publish a terrorist novel, you have got to make terrorism much more consequential than it really is. In the novel, terrorism has got to change the world in some big way—breaking up a peace conference that could end the Middle East conflict, for instance—or otherwise you simply don't have a novel that is going to grip its readers. At least so far as terrorist thrillers are concerned, therefore, the time is past when it was enough just to catch a murderer who had killed only one single little unimportant human being.

Terrorism, here, must therefore be magnified beyond any resemblance to its historical achievement (or, rather, lack of achievement) before it can be made into the subject of a novel; failing that, terrorism is of no interest to the general public.

These orientations, then, were part of de Mille's marching orders. Some further directions were also included in the package. Carefully emphasizing that most of his editors were Jewish, de Mille said that they had pointed out to him that the Arabs *do* have a cause, that they are *not* clowns, and that they ought to be treated more evenhandedly than they ordinarily are in modern fiction. In *Paradise Lost,* de Mille reminded me, Milton gave Satan three times the coverage that he allotted to the Good Lord. De Mille remarked that while he tried to follow these instructions, he could not please everyone. Mordecai Richler, a member of the editorial board of the Book-of-the-Month Club, would have liked to see the Arabs dealt with better than they are in *By the Rivers of Babylon.* According to de Mille, Richler felt they came across as pure bad guys, which, de Mille said, "was not our intention."

I pointed out that in fact both sets of people—Arabs and Israelis alike—come across as rather unattractive, and that there is really no unequivocally heroic figure in the book. (The character who comes closest to being a hero is the El Al security chief, who, as already mentioned, is aptly described as a Nazi by one of his companions.)

De Mille explained this readily. "You need great times to have heroes," he said, "and we haven't seen such days since World War II." I asked him whether he had any heroes. He thought about that for a while and then said that yes, perhaps he could consider that Russian author a hero, but he couldn't quite remember his name just now. "Solzhenitsyn?" I suggested. "Yes," de Mille replied. "That's the one."

We talked about politics. De Mille said that he used to be a liberal but that he does not see himself as that any longer. He doesn't quite know how he would describe his political views now, but they would be approximately in the area of libertarianism, which is to say resisting governmental encroachment and supporting the tax revolt.

He went on to say that men are violent by nature and that there is no escaping this fact. At high school he loved playing football, and he could still recall now the real satisfaction kicking people's heads in gave him in the game. He was drafted and assigned to Fort Benning, Georgia, but garrison duty there became pretty boring, so he volunteered for service in Vietnam.

He told me that he figures his violence now is fairly well sublimated by writing and by supporting the tax-revolt movement. But that, he speculated, may have a lot to do with the fact that he is not quite as young as he used to be (he is thirty-four now), and with testosterone levels and that kind of thing. He lives pretty much the kind of life he wants to, but even now he thinks that boredom is a real problem. Affluence generates monotony, he explained; media hype wears every sensation out almost instantaneously; and he reckons that if monotony is a problem for him, it must be ten times more of a problem for people living dull little nine-to-five lives—and even more of a problem for the somewhat younger people who have never experienced a real war.

"War is exciting, you've got to admit that," de Mille said. Even now, he pointed out, there are old men around who can go on forever retelling stories about their World War II experiences; and while Vietnam is not something people who were there like to discuss with people who were not, veterans of that war can't resist telling each other their war stories. "I even know people who lost their arms, or legs, or were terribly wounded in other ways, and they insist that the Vietnam war was the most exciting time in their lives."

Violence is in our nature and war is exciting: "There's hardly an anti–Vietnam war liberal I know whose children don't play with rifles or *Star Wars* laser beams or swords or whatever," de Mille remarked. And he added, "We tend to think we're living in pretty troubled times nowadays, but I've no doubt that when the history books are written, people will look at our period and see that it was a very tranquil time—an interlude."

De Mille believes that we are unconsciously gearing up for war—a big, exciting war that all the people will support enthusiastically. He thinks we are too soft with our opponents and with the Third World countries, and that it is not going to be long before the people will be fed up with all that and will demand some dramatic, large-scale military action. "There hasn't been a real war since 1945," he said, "and people are so hooked on that one they continue to read hundreds of books and go to all sorts of movies about it."

And this, he went on to speculate, is how the fascination with terrorism fits in. In part, of course, that fascination has to do with people's hostility to government. Everyone is fed up with government these days. The middle class and the rich because government is taking away too much from them, and the poor because government is not giving enough to them. Terrorism is antigovernment and therefore gratifying, potentially, to almost everyone.

Terrorism also counters boredom—the monotony of our dull, affluent world. De Mille cited a terrorist thriller called *The Red Madonna,* whose heroine joins the IRA because she finds her life as a factory girl in Belfast too boring to tolerate any longer. This brings her back to square one, where the real problem of human survival can be experienced. Now, of course, life is no longer boring for her. De Mille suggested that this woman reflects a lot of the needs that attract people to terrorism today.

Most important, though, de Mille thought that terrorism represents some sort of preliminary, brushfire wars that before long will produce the real thing. Terrorist episodes, in this sense, are a bit like what the Spanish Civil War or the Ethiopian War were to World War II. Terrorism satisfies some of the human need for violence and excitement but, because it does not satisfy it adequately, tends to whet the appetite all the more.

De Mille did not seem unduly perturbed by this prediction. "You rationalize away fear by saying it can't happen to me," he said, recalling his days in Vietnam.

Waiting for the train back to New York City, we talked about books we would like to write. I confessed that my unmarketable proposition was a book about the Taj Mahal, a nice big coffee-table book full of gorgeous full-color photographs ("The Taj by moonlight from a helicopter"), and an introductory essay describing, among other things, the role played by Italian architects and craftsmen in constructing the monument. De Mille's unpublishable project is based on an incident he observed in Vietnam. A forty-year-old sergeant had stepped on a land mine, which blew away his legs, arms, and testicles. The company medic, a conscientious objector, summoned the medivac helicopter and gave the injured man a shot of morphine. A lieutenant demanded that he give him a further shot.

"It would kill him at once!" the medic objected.

"He's lost so much blood he can barely take the dose I've just given him!"

The medivac helicopter was already in earshot when the lieutenant grabbed a vial of morphine and injected it into the wounded soldier. Death was almost instantaneous.

Soon after, the medic filed charges against the lieutenant. The officer was given a choice of having a strongly negative letter placed in his file, which would effectively put an end to his military career, or of facing a court-martial on a charge of manslaughter. He opted for the former.

In de Mille's novel, however, he would have chosen to stand trial. The novel would have explored the themes of mercy killing, masculinity, and the making of decisions under enormous stress.

As the train pulled into the station, I said I hoped de Mille would one day get a chance to write that book. If he does, and if it is as good as *By the Rivers of Babylon*, it will be a fine work.

Bernard Geis, copublisher of *By the Rivers*, and the man who first conceived the novel, spared me some moments for a quick interview over the telephone. He said the idea had come to him from Franz Werfel's *Forty Days of Musa Dagh*, a novel in which Armenian refugees on a mountaintop fight off the Turks who are trying to kill them. The most dramatic military episodes, Mr. Geis said, are those involving sieges, and he wanted Nelson de Mille to write a good siege novel.

"Isn't it a *terrorist* novel, though?" I asked.

"No," Geis replied, "it's a siege novel."

He went on to say that the head of one of the very

large paperback publishing houses had told him that this was not an Arab-Israeli book but a cops-and-robbers one.

All this struck me as very odd. The dust jacket of the book shows an arm with a crumpled Concorde clutched in its fist; the arm is tattooed with an Arabic inscription saying something like "free Palestine."

"Terrorist novels," Geis hastened to say, "succeed despite the terrorist action. People don't like to read about terrorism any more than they like to read about cancer."

Then he said that terrorism is not a plus for *By the Rivers of Babylon,* and again repeated that it was a siege novel. With that the interview ended.

Now, I don't want to imply that this is not, in some respects, a siege novel, but it seems absurd to deny that it is a terrorist novel more than it is anything else.

A curious insight on the matter of realism, so called, in terrorist novels: Throughout the book the Concordes are identified as belonging to El Al, the Israeli national airline. The crumpled plane on the dust-jacket illustration is painted in El Al's distinctive blue and white colors and has the "4X" designation which is the registration prefix for Israeli civilian aircraft. However, El Al's name does not appear on either the fuselage or tail of the aircraft, and neither does its Star of David logo. This, Nelson de Mille led me to understand, was a decision reached by the publishers in order not to offend the Israeli airline . . .

. . . which might otherwise think that this is a terrorist novel?

Backed by several billion dollars from the Chinese communists, a beautiful and brilliant black woman named Agatha Teel secretly gains control over the heroin and gambling networks that crisscross the United States. From this base, she plans to launch simultaneous uprisings in thirty major cities. The civil war this will spark off will lead to the downfall of the republic. The authorities learn that some colossal plot is afoot, but they are not sure of its details. The novel ends when the government's principal investigator, severely wounded by one of the plotters, telephones his office and reports that he has discovered who the ringleader is. He gives the name of a prominent U.S. senator and then falls dead. The senator is entirely innocent. Agatha Teel remains free to implement her plans.

The author of the spellbinding novel *Whisper of the Axe,* in which this tale is told, is Richard Condon. Although Condon is best known for his *Manchurian Candidate, Whisper of the Axe* is a remarkably gripping work and was a considerable commercial success, selling three-quarters of a million copies in the paperback edition.

Terrorism was very much on my mind one hot July afternoon when I went to call on Condon in his splendid Georgian mansion some hundred miles south of Dublin. Changing planes at London's Heathrow Airport, I watched as a cordon of tanks, armored cars, and heavily armed troops was deployed to protect the Israeli and Egyptian foreign ministers from a PLO attack as they arrived for a peace conference under the auspices of the American secretary of state. Two hours later, I was driving along Dublin's North Circular Road when my car was halted by the police so that a small but very dangerous-looking convoy bristling with machine guns could speed by on its way to delivering a captured IRA terrorist to the local prison. And then on past Phoenix Park . . .

"I shouldn't have written *Whisper of the Axe,*" Condon told me at the very outset of our conversation —and then went on to describe why he did write it and what was at the back of his mind when he did so. The United States, he pointed out, has so far avoided having a war fought on its own soil. Yet the law of averages, if nothing else, makes it seem inevitable to Condon that sooner or later a major military conflict will take place here. This will not be a conventional war, however, but an internal one—a civil war.

The social upheavals of our period make this seem logical, according to Condon. We are living in jagged and hopelessly fragmented times, he said, and not only the 73 percent of the people who are under thirty, but blacks and other minorities who have good reason to be discontented are in rebellion against the status quo. This rebellion makes terrorism seem attractive to far more people than just the handful who become terrorists.

"But, you know," Condon said vigorously, "if you think terrorism is a romantic ideal of a group of Robin Hoods who are giving up the best years of their lives in order to bring us all pie in the sky in the shape of better government, you are out of your fucking mind.

"What's really going on, what makes people rebellious and attracted to terrorism and to all kinds of other destructive, violent endeavors, is just what was predicted by a Regius Professor of Natural History at the University of Aberdeen, in Scotland. Whenever the food-supply system becomes threatened, the species decimates itself so that its food supply will be sufficient for those who survive.

"We have enormously high crime rates, soaring homosexuality threatening reproduction, wars, disease —all in an unconscious effort to decimate the population so that the food supply will be made safe.

"Throwing all this together, I decided that the way I could show people what is happening and will continue to happen is through a melodrama involving urban guerrilla warfare in thirty key cities in the United States. And I say I shouldn't have written this novel, because it wasn't necessary. The whole natural prerogative of our biology is taking us to that point anyway."

He laughed—a disturbing, almost triumphant laugh. "These things," he continued, "had to happen in the West. In traditional societies like India they had all sorts of religious protections to allow everybody to live out their lives, short as these were, in disease and hopelessness. We've gotten rid of those, created enormous expectations, and have even gone a long way toward meeting them—but at a cost that we cannot pay. In a very real sense, food is much more seriously threatened in the West than anywhere else because we depend so heavily on the machine to produce it and on massive corporations to bring it to us. The fuel crisis is crippling our machines, the shortage of capital, soaring interest rates, and so on, are restricting the corporations, and the result is such dramatic increases in the price of food that people can't afford to eat at home any longer: which is why all those garbage fast-food places have struck it rich."

There are, he went on to say, colossal forces at work in nature that are pushing us in the same direction—the direction of decimating the species. "In 1982, three planets will be lined up with the sun," Condon explained, quoting a report he had read in *Newsweek.* "And when this happens, there will be some interference with magnetic waves, which will have a fantastic seismological effect on the great geological faults. In 1982, there are going to be huge earthquakes all over the world. These will be as destructive as two thousand hydrogen bombs and, believe me, they are going to have devastating consequences for technology and population size alike."

He paused and gave a slightly apologetic shrug. "When I talk like this, I sound like a crackpot to myself. But what I really am saying is that man and nature are conspiring to limit the problem of feeding our species."

"But you don't seem in the least bit alarmed by all this," I pointed out. "Why is that?"

"Well," Condon replied, "I believe in the logical, unemotional acceptance of the fact that this is a condition which neither I nor you nor any combination of people can alter—part of a great forward march of the species in the geophysical evolution of the planet. And terrorism contributes to it all, of course."

"In *Whisper of the Axe,*" I said, "the story unfolds very much from Agatha Teel's perspective. Is she the heroine—despite the fact that she's the villain?"

"From John F. Kennedy through Richard Nixon

and Gerald Ford and Jimmy Carter, we have had only negative heroes," he answered. "They are totally negative people; their accomplishments are negative and they are morbid heroes. Every one of them is so flawed that you could almost consider him diseased. So, of course, Agatha Teel is a negative force, but that is because we are in an interregnum—a pause between two great historical eras of innocence and enlightenment— in which only negative forces can be recognized. What attracts the masses, the collective mind, is negative aspirations and achievements."

"And is that what attracts you, too?" I asked.

"I don't really look at myself in those terms," he said. "But when I set out to do the work that I do, I do it with a sense of acceptance that this is the center of the sun. I want to be read, and at the same time I seek to get further into the core of things."

"Do you really think that our past few presidents —from Kennedy on—*are* regarded as heroes? It seems to me that they all, even Kennedy nowadays, are regarded with a lot of mistrust. People tend rather to dislike them."

"But sixty-seven thousand copies of John Ehrlichman's novel—*The Company*—were sold in hardcover, and that's a very, very healthy sale. Didn't they also make a TV movie of it? My new novel is about Nixon, and I wrote it out of what I believe is on the reader's part a deep and abiding sense of envy of every one of his qualities: He's corrupt and very, very rich. I think the man has about three hundred million dollars. I'm so around the bend on this that I think Nixon put up the money for his advance to get cash on his book.

PART TWO

12/Terrorism and Terrorist Chic

THE INSIGNIFICANCE OF TERRORISM STANDS in remarkable contrast to the attention we pay it. Watching the gory spectacles brought to us live and in full color on TV, or reading the newspaper reports or the proliferation of books and scholarly studies on the subject (there is now even an academic journal devoted exclusively to reporting research on terrorism), one might be forgiven the impression that the barbarians are at the gates of Rome.

That is not the case, of course, and almost certainly never could be. Despite the availability of modern weapons and of sanctuaries in which to hide—and also despite the vulnerability of our densely packed cities—terrorists have proven to be remarkably impotent. A sober examination establishes that terrorists have caused very little destruction of either life or property, and that the political consequences of their assaults are negligible. No regime has fallen to terrorist attack, and no significant social, political, or economic changes have been brought about as a result of terrorist pressure.[1]

This consideration would be profoundly dispiriting to terrorists if they really were concerned about attaining political objectives. Terrorism is not, however, in any reasonable sense of the term, a political activity. The concepts of rationality and purpose that we apply in political analysis have no place in a discussion of terrorism—except by way of calling attention to the conclusion, surprising but inescapable, that *terrorism is profoundly purposeless and irrational.*[2]

Under the flamboyant and self-righteous rhetoric of terrorist ideology and proclamation, two qualities stand out. "Terrorism feels and never reasons, and therefore is always right." Emerson's remark captures

---

[1] The view of terrorism suggested here owes much to Walter Laqueur, *Terrorism* (Boston: Little, Brown, 1977), an eminently sensible, myth-shattering study that is surely the best analysis of terrorism currently available.

[2] One indication of terrorism's irrationality may be found in the tenuous connection between terrorist deeds and the goals they are ostensibly designed to serve. This lack of connection, in turn, owes much to the vagueness of many terrorist goals. It is all very well to say that one wishes to destroy imperialism, or racism, or whatever. But where do these alleged evils reside? One does not want to attack manifestations of them, merely, but the essence of the evil itself. And this—the evil, as such—is usually not assailable by force of arms for the very obvious reason that its locus cannot be ascertained.

perfectly the subjectivity and purposelessness of terrorism—and thus not only its unwillingness to deal with reality but its monumental capacity for inhumanity.

"Qu'importe les victimes si le geste est beau?" [What do the victims matter if the deed is beautiful?] was the epigram of Laurent Tailhade, a sympathizer rather than an actual terrorist, and his appreciation of the beautiful deed may have been diminished somewhat when he lost the sight of an eye as a result of a terrorist attack. Nevertheless, his *bon mot* fits well the self-sufficient joy of murder and destruction that underlies the terrorist mentality. "The terrorist despises all dogmas and all sciences," Nechayeff, the nineteenth-century Russian terrorist, declared. "He knows only one science—the science of destruction."

There is no purpose in this, no contribution to the attainment of the revolution, but simply—and almost sufficiently—the enjoyment of disgustingly meaningless brutality. Even terrorism's pseudorationality expresses the terrorist's disdain for human life. From Emile Henry's "There are no innocents" to the PLO's "How can you say who is and who is not a combatant?"[3] it provides license for indiscriminate and *meaningless* slaughter and destruction.

There are no ideas, then, to be conveyed by terrorism's "propaganda of the deed," only an angry, senseless lashing out at the world in which the terrorist feels discontented.

---

[3] Jan Schreiber, *The Ultimate Weapon: Terrorists and World Order* (New York: William Morrow, 1978), p. 137.

Mitigating terrorism's brutality in a practical sense, but perhaps compounding it in a political one, is the feebleness of terrorism, its impotence—even its laziness. (During the four years 1971 to 1975, one of America's most notorious terrorist groups, the Weather Underground, averaged one-sixth of an attack per person per year!)[4]

Terrorism, therefore, is not a specter that ought —objectively—to haunt us. But it is a spectacle to which we are compulsively drawn. Max Lerner has called terrorism "one of the nightmare problems of our time"— a significant metaphor this, even if not in the sense he intended. For what is a nightmare but a phantasm that does *not* exist in reality and has its roots in the prohibited but nevertheless persistent impulses of the unconscious mind?

Perhaps it was also an unwitting slip that led another scholar, Jan Schreiber, to write that terrorism's "popularity . . . works."[5] Be that as it may, there can be little doubt that in some curious sense terrorism

---

[4] *Osawatomie* (Summer 1975, no. 2), a Weather Underground publication reprinted in *Terroristic Activity,* Hearings before the . . . Committee on the Judiciary of the United States Senate, Part 7, Oct. 23, 1975, p. 540, cites the "25 armed actions against the enemy" carried out in four years. A staff report, *The Weather Underground,* for the same committee, lists thirty-seven men and women as active in the group as of 1975. In fact, membership in the Weather Underground was probably larger in the early years of the decade.

[5] Schreiber, *The Ultimate Weapon,* p. 198. Lerner's remark quoted above is part of the flap copy for Schreiber's book.

is popular and that we are fascinated by it for reasons which have nothing to do with the actuality of terrorism's threat—negligible as that is—to the world.

Our interest in terrorism, I suggest, is far more interesting than terrorism itself, though it could well be that the irrationality which shapes our perceptions of it is closely tied to the irrationality which shapes terrorism itself.

"Terrorism ultimately aims at the spectator," Dr. F. Gentry Harris, a psychiatrist who has studied terrorism closely, notes. "The victim is secondary," he goes on to say. "Death, destruction of property, the flamboyant or dangerous use of technological devices, deprivation of liberty, are not ends of terrorism. They are means by which to terrorize—to make an impression on the spectator."[6]

The terrorist cannot act in a vacuum. He needs an audience to observe his actions, to be shocked and terrified by them. Why this is so must remain a matter for speculation. Could it be that the terrorist is so lacking in the capacity for feeling—perhaps, as someone once said, he is so *bored*—that he needs to create a sense of shock in others if he is to feel it in himself?

But for whatever reason, the terrorist needs his audience. And he gets it. Perhaps it would be going too far to say that if terrorism did not exist, we would have had to invent it, but in significant measure we have indeed invented terrorism. The terrorist performs by

---

[6] *Terrorism,* Hearings before the Committee on Internal Security, House of Representatives, Part I, Feb.–March 1974, pp. 2954 ff.

popular demand, just like any other actor, and is no less aware of his audience—of us—than we are of him. "Terrorism has unfortunately become a form of mass entertainment," Dr. Frederick Hacker notes. "If one could cut out the publicity, I would say you could cut out 75 percent of the national and international terrorism."[7]

This is not the old epistemological crux, translated into modern terms, of the tree falling unseen and unheard in the forest ("has it fallen?"). Terrorism *would* vanish if no one paid attention to it, just as surely as a Broadway play would close if no one bought tickets to see it.

The terrorists' "propaganda of the deed," like all propaganda that is successful, falls on receptive ears. We are responsive to this propaganda, we take the terrorists seriously—and we provide them with means for communicating their propaganda to us.

Here are some examples of how we help propagate the terrorist message. In November 1977, *The New York Times Magazine* carried an article about the latest Paris fashions. Two of the less well-known couturiers, the article reported, "both sent out models in faintly threatening, black leather, nail-studded outfits and Nazi-style caps—a cross between the punk and neo-Nazi movements stirring in Europe. Fortunately, their provocative gesture does not appear to herald a trend; none of the big designers made a bow in that direction. Nevertheless, these 'terrorist' statements registered—which is one of the reasons these new tal-

<hr>
[7] Ibid., p. 3039.

which the terrorists are playing is not only made up of people who avidly read sensationalized news reports of the latest terrorist act. No less, the audience comprises people who entertain themselves with "terrorist statements" of all kinds, and find excitement and pleasure in the fantasies those statements embody.

Terrorist Chic is not merely another expression of the perennial fascination of our species in general, or of American society in particular, with violence. Terrorist Chic does not merge with other, more familiar types of violence. We do not glorify street crimes or automobile accidents, though they may well have a certain fascination for us. Our appetites for Westerns and war movies and detective stories, for boxing matches and other violent sports, by the same token, seem to exist independently of the impulses gratified by Terrorist Chic, and they have, in any case, quite different historical origins.

On the other hand, it is clear that the advent of Terrorist Chic does *not* mean that our fashion designers and models, our singers and photographers, our sexual adventurers and novelists, are on the verge of joining the international brotherhood of terrorists. Nor do I think that the millions who thrill to the provocations of terrorists and the purveyors of Terrorist Chic alike are about to start shooting at us and blowing us up and kidnapping us in order to save us from fascism, imperialism, and every other imaginable evil.

Terrorist Chic shows that we are attracted and excited by the fantasies which motivate the terrorists themselves. But just as we are not willing to suppress those fantasies, or to confine them to purely private spheres, so too are we unwilling to act them out in the way terrorists do. Terrorist Chic is thus the outer limit society is able to allow itself in expressing the fantasies which terrorists themselves make explicit through their behavior. It is a way of playing terrorism in which no one gets hurt—rather as small boys play cowboys and Indians.

Earlier, I suggested that the irrationality which shapes our perception of terrorism may be linked to the irrationality which shapes terrorism itself. At that point, I was referring to the extent to which the threat posed by terrorists, and the political significance of terrorism, are exaggerated in the popular mind. The artifacts and manners of Terrorist Chic show that we are indeed caught up by the terrorist fantasy. It is therefore quite probable that it is these fantasies, to which we subscribe, that shape our overestimation of terrorism.

Freud speculated (in *Group Psychology and the Analysis of the Ego*) that groups of people share and are held together by a set of unconscious psychological needs; the leader of the group also possesses these needs, perhaps to a heightened degree, and shows his followers the way in which their needs may be gratified. This construct has been applied by scholars in numerous instances to the study of groups, and perhaps more than any other single formulation underlies the study of group psychology. Freud's theory, however, can quite profitably be extended beyond the study of groups and their leaders as conventionally defined. The fans of a baseball team, for example, are joined to each other and to the team itself by shared unconscious needs, which the team must fulfill if it is to retain the fans' loyalty. In much the same way, those of us who are irrational in our perceptions of terrorism and find excitement in the posturings of Terrorist Chic are joined to each other and to the terrorists themselves by shared unconscious needs. As long as the terrorists are fulfilling those needs, we will remain loyal—albeit covertly loyal—to them. Part of the task facing the terrorist, of course, is to act in such a way that his audience (his followers, in this sense) finds gratification in his deeds.

What actually are the needs that seek gratification through terrorism? Since the lust for destruction seems to be the most salient characteristic of terrorism, we may be tempted to assume that it is this that attracts us, and terrorists themselves.

But a number of considerations argue against such an assumption. The rhetoric of terrorists is almost always far more frightening than their actual deeds: The resounding calls to arms, the chilling threats are followed only by the relatively minor and sporadic attacks that terrorists actually carry out. Some of these are dramatic, to be sure, and some of them result in a tragic loss of life. Nevertheless, the damage caused by terrorists is negligible in comparison with their potential and their avowed intentions.

Why is the terrorist so ineffectual—almost, so lazy? Why, to paraphrase the Symbionese Liberation Army, does the single running man not slit a thousand throats in one night?[8] Part of the explanation may lie in the effectiveness of defense measures against terrorism, but it would be fatuous to argue that these shield us in any significant way from determined terrorist attack. Even in a police state, society is extremely vulnerable to the terrorist; in a democratic political system, there is almost no limit to the number of major targets a terrorist might assault. And yet—the terrorist remains curiously ineffective and inactive. Could it be that he is, in fact, only *playing* at being a terrorist?

We have seen that much of the sadomasochism flaunted by Terrorist Chic is actually quite phony. The regalia are only decorative; the posturing is just that, and reflects neither commitment nor practice. Just as Terrorist Chic plays at terrorism, so too does it play at sadomasochism.

The real task for us, however, is to understand what prompts all this playing with images of evil and brutality. The particular nature of this play indicates, of course, that those engaged in it are giving vent to a great deal of pent-up hostility and aggression. Why do they feel so hostile and aggressive?

The image-makers of Terrorist Chic whom we have met in this book fall into three categories. One group comprises people who, while quite talented, appear to be unbalanced by sadomasochistic and/or paranoid qualities. For them, the advent of Terrorist Chic is indeed a much welcomed opportunity to bring their deviance out of the closet, and to have it validated and acclaimed by others.

---

[8]   *Terroristic Activity,* p. 559.

A second group is merely opportunistic; these people are as willing to cash in on Terrorist Chic as they would be on any other trend that comes along.

The largest group, however, and the one most directly responsible for establishing Terrorist Chic as a fashionable public pose, is driven by very different impulses.

Many in this group had been active in the peace movement in the 1960s or had been VISTA volunteers or had entered the Catholic novitiate. Now, in the seventies, they have flip-flopped to the opposite extreme, substituting callowness, violence, and a trite fascination with evil for their earlier high idealism.

But already these same individuals are preparing themselves to abandon Terrorist Chic and move on into new areas. One person told me he was "into finding inner peace"; another is now searching for tenderness; yet another for beauty and purity of form.

Terrorist Chic, in other words, will soon be *passé.* In a couple of years it will have faded into oblivion, leaving the opportunists to search for new pastures and the authentic deviants to find their way back into their closets.

Whatever replaces Terrorist Chic, though, will be just as ephemeral for most of its practitioners as Terrorist Chic itself has been. "One gets bored with everything," Robert Currie told me. "I feel free to try out whatever comes along. I'm not creating a life-style that's permanent for me."

These remarks, far more than any arrogant and reckless paean to violence and destruction, sound the leitmotiv of Terrorist Chic; and they also identify the needs that have shaped terrorism itself. Currie had spoken of his need incessantly to tear himself away from whatever is routine and ordinary. This need had led him, in the span of a few years, from antiwar activism, VISTA, and the Catholic church to the "depravity" (as he called it) of Terrorist Chic, and now it was carrying him to his newest enthusiasm—"Beauty: That's where my head is at." For Currie, terrorists are fascinating because they too step out of the ordinary routine of life and do things which run-of-the-mill people do not.

If this urge—or something akin to it—is what makes terrorism fascinating to the bystander, it is, I think, also the impulse which propels men and women into careers of terrorism. We recall that Susan Sontag described the aesthete's subversion as the antidote to life as a bore; in fact, at least since Tocqueville, extreme behavior and beliefs have been seen as a way of escaping from the oppressive monotony of middle-class life and affluence.

But is it boredom, really, that underlies these postures and acts? "It's not the terrorist deed but everything that leads up to it, not the act but its anticipation, that I find fascinating," Robert Currie had also remarked. "Once the act is done, it's over, and you have to go on to something else."

One is bored with something when one has had too much of it—and that does not seem to be quite what Currie and so many others in this book are really talking about. Rather, the problem appears to lie in a direction that is slightly, but significantly, different. For what these people are saying, in effect, is that experience is inferior to the anticipation of it, and that it does not represent the fulfillment of expectations but their inevitable debasement. Hence, the endlessly shifting flow of commitments and enthusiasms which we have noted in them, the effortless and casual way in which they are adopted and discarded. And hence too, I suspect, the strangely lackadaisical and ineffective quality of terrorism which we have noted. If anticipating— planning—an act is so much more rewarding than executing it, the terrorist's impulse to act and be effective is necessarily going to be undermined.

The condition that we are talking about therefore does not appear to be one of boredom or surfeit. The men and women who people the pages of this book are not gluttons but anorectics. The food is there—in fact, in abundance unmatched in history—but they cannot get any nourishment from it. Indeed, they cannot really eat it.

They suffer from anorexia of experience: This, I believe, is the heart of the matter. Christopher Makos spoke of trying to forget everything, and of not having any memory. He said this was the price he had to pay for waking up "new" every morning. The truth, though, is the reverse of what he appears to believe. Waking up "new" every morning is the price he has to pay for not really remembering anything; that is, for not really experiencing anything. For all his braggadocio, one of Makos's biggest difficulties in life is staying awake. "I'm always searching for new things and new people to keep me awake," he told me; and "I like to have things poking at me, and making me feel, like, Christopher, wake up, you're alive!"

He finds these stimuli in abundance—after all, he inhabits one of the centers of New York cultural life —only to encounter a hopeless dilemma. For while he needs these stimuli to make him feel alive and awake, the more he obtains of them the less alive and awake he actually feels, and he ends up, as he expressed it, being "lulled" and "hypnotized" by them. Tragically, he has no choice *but* to wake up "new" every morning, for the wonderfully rich diversity of experiences he has encountered the previous day have not really touched him except as a soporific. In the end, like so many others, he must resort to the most radical therapy: "Sometimes I let myself be beaten. . . . It wakes me out of a zombie state."

Many years ago, Theodor Reik suggested that what the masochist enjoys is not the pain but the fact that he is experiencing *something*. Terrorist Chic is indeed a zombie's posture—the posture, that is to say, of people who cannot experience much because they cannot commit themselves to anything. They are driven to their sensational conduct by their quest for sensation. Under the circumstances, one might be tempted to welcome their sadomasochism: "If this is what the zombies need to come awake, then by all means . . ."

However, precisely the needs which have led them to this extreme make it difficult or impossible for them to acquire the benefits which sadomasochism might be able to provide. There is, after all, no reason to suppose that those who encounter experience in general as the debasement of expectation will be able to approach this particular experience in a different way. And, as we saw repeatedly in the preceding chapters, this is indeed the case. Even some of the most overt sadomasochism of Terrorist Chic turns out, on inquiry, to be phony and nothing more than mere posturing.

From one point of view, all this is, of course, quite reassuring; we are glad to know that the practitioners of Terrorist Chic are not really going to hurt themselves or others, and we are relieved to discover that terrorists themselves are almost congenitally incapable of being particularly effective. And just as the former are already getting bored with their new style, so too can we expect that the terrorists will tire of their adventures. (If nothing else, our growing lack of interest in terrorism will also serve to discourage them.)

From another point of view, however, this situation is deeply unsettling. The terrorists, and Terrorist Chic too, now appear as products of a phenomenon far more dangerous than the boredom engendered by bourgeois monotony and affluence, merely. Boredom can be appeased by something interesting. *The incapacity to find anything interesting*—that is to say, the incapacity to experience—is, however, a condition for which no remedy appears available. Boredom may be a product of the industrial revolution. The condition we are talking about here, though, is a product of postindustrial society—of modernity.

Modernity is marked by rapidly accelerating rates of change and by the no less rapid proliferation of choices concerning almost everything that fills our lives. In this kaleidoscopic world, it is increasingly difficult for us to hold on to anything that makes us feel rooted and real. Our preferences, our bonds to others, even our sense of ourselves are threatened with evanescence and superficiality. No sooner do we opt for one choice than a myriad of new ones comes along to entice us away from it. Everything, it seems, is becoming instantly acquirable and instantly disposable.

The people we have met in this book exemplify this way of being. We see from their example that the consequence of a willingness to encounter everything is that you experience nothing. A life that careens wildly from one posture to the next is not enriched by any of them; the self does not grow as a result, but sinks into a deepening promiscuity of being. There is no authentic gratification in this mode of being, but only a combination of listlessness, triviality, identity confusion, and an unappeasable need for sensation, which—in the more conventional sense of the word—does indeed result in promiscuity. And the trouble with promiscuity is not that it is "immoral" so much as that it vitiates the self and robs life by making experience negligible. Where there is no commitment, there can be no real experience, and then, indeed, it becomes necessary to say, "Nothing is real" and "I can get no satisfaction."

What will the outcome of all this be? Words like "beauty," "harmony," "tenderness," and "love" are being bandied about by the conquistadores of Terrorist Chic to identify the directions in which they are now heading. This cluster of orientations may well herald tomorrow's trend—the things that we will be "into" for a while. But I doubt whether they will be around for long, if indeed they actually materialize.

For, of course, the fascination with violence and destruction, while largely a sadomasochistic quest for sensation (as I have argued), is also aggressive in the more literal sense. The people we are looking at here are not only bewildered at the surfeit of choices available to them and the transitory nature of each of them; they do not only feel disenchanted with life's possibilities. They are, in a sense, spoiled. But it is also true that life has been spoiled for them, and that they are very, very angry at that fact. They need kicks; *but they also need to kick.*

It is from this perspective that it becomes particularly necessary to recognize the hippies as the precursors of both terrorism and Terrorist Chic. The hippies were pampered, overindulged, disenchanted kids who sought radical remedies to infuse themselves with excitement and purpose, and who also felt rage at the world which was depriving them by offering them so much.[9]

---

[9]   A rereading of hippie literature from the 1960s and early 1970s establishes the extraordinary extent of the counterculture's preoccupation with the alleged destructiveness of bourgeois society. This preoccupation is expressed in language that is often hysterical and paranoid in tone and certainly overstates the case greatly. Even such a relatively "moderate" hippie book as *The Greening of America*—written by a Yale Law School professor—is marked by these characteristics.

More notable, though, is the fact that the remedies suggested by the hippies sound suspiciously like the evils they are designed to counteract. The hippie emphasis on the value of subjectivity and spontaneity, for example, is more destructive of community, friendship, and love relations than anything "straight" society could dream up.

A footnote is hardly the place to explore so significant

The hippies were no less the victims of modernity than their successors (large numbers of whom in fact came from hippie culture). They too suffered from modernity's anorexia of experience, and life for them was a seemingly endless escalation of ungratifying highs, of enthusiasms and commitments and styles adopted and abandoned effortlessly and carelessly. But the hippies were the love generation, so called; and while there was a great deal of hostility toward society just beneath the surface of their culture, the fact is that for the most part their aggression remained buried and unrecognized.

It is not impossible, indeed, that all the talk of love and peace to which the hippies were addicted may have hastened the demise of their culture in favor of a life-style that *could* express the underlying aggression. Be that as it may; but while the hippies' quest for sensation was carried forward in Terrorist Chic and in terrorism, their aggression was radically transformed in the sense that it now surfaced and became quite explicit.

This means that whatever follows from Terrorist Chic will not only have to represent a continuing—and doomed—quest for sensation, but will also have to embody the aggression it has inherited from its forebears. This aggression, to repeat, has its roots in the rage felt

---

a topic, and I will confine myself here merely to voicing the suggestion that the hippie diagnosis of bourgeois America may actually have been a covert, unconscious expression of the destructiveness the hippies themselves sought to express.

toward the world for bringing about the "anorexia of experience."

Possibly this aggression will once again become sublimated and buried as it was in the hippies' culture. There are many signs, though, for those who care to read them, that we may be heading in a quite different direction instead. In *Civilization and Its Discontents,* Freud had argued that war is a form of rebellion against the repression of our instincts which civilization mandates. Our problem, however, is not the repression of instincts so much as their almost limitless gratification, to the point where gratification itself becomes vitiated. Could it be that war may also arise to protest, not the repressions of civilization—but its indulgences? Rather in the way that the individual, yearning for sensation, turns to sadomasochism so that he can at last experience something, might not an entire society turn to war? War, of course, is nothing if not real. Will it prove to be the only real experience left?

Recently, the newspapers carried an advertisement for Gimbels, one of the least chic New York department stores, that featured three women in pseudomilitary clothing, this being one of the new fashion "bombs" of the season. The banner headline declared: "Suddenly . . . It's Me!" " 'Cause when I'm in a military mood, I'm one super little trooper," part of the accompanying text read.

As I was standing by the dance floor of Studio 54, the thought occurred to me, "It's been a long time since these people have had a lovely war." Quite coincidentally, a few days later David Richmond (coauthor of *The Passion of Dracula*) told me of a remark once made to him by an old vaudevillian: "People always dance before a war," he had said. Shortly thereafter, I spoke with Nelson de Mille, who told me that terrorism is "like one of those little brush wars before a really big one starts up. It won't be long now . . ."

Is this—"a really big war"—going to be our next thrill?

And will it be our last one?

Index

Index

Index

Holstrom, John, 117–120
Homosexuals and homosexuality, 5, 19, 172
  bars, 7, 8, 10, 11
  Christopher and West streets, 5–12
  leather attire, 10
  "novelties only" stores, 6–9, 11–12
  sadomasochism, 8, 9–10, 11
Hot Knives (punk rock group), 113
Hussein, King, 48

I Am Sick (punk rock group), 113
Impeccable Warrior Store, The, 6–7
Interview (magazine), 129
Introductory Lectures on Psychoanalysis, The (Freud), 43–44
Irish Republican Army (IRA), 158, 163, 168, 184

Jagger, Mick, 52, 57
James Bond (character), 28, 151, 152
Jencks, Charles, 64
Jerks, The (punk rock group), 113
Jews, 92–93
Johnson, Philip, 5
Jones, Grace, 75

Kafka, Franz, 16
Keller, Marthe, 154–155
Kennedy, John F., 170–171

Killer (punk rock album), 113
"Killer, The" (shoe advertisement), 27, 39, 40
Kill Me (punk rock song title), 113
Kinks (punk rock group), 113
KISS albums, 108–109
Kitt, Eartha, 52, 54
Klein, Gene. *See* Simmons, Gene
Kong-Ress (punk rock group), 113
Kosinski, Jerzy, 103–106

Laing, R. D., 91–92
Lansbury, Angela, 53
Laqueur, Walter, 178
Leather and leather jackets, 75, 80, 81, 96, 98, 100, 149, 182
Le Corbusier, 5
Lerner, Max, 180
Liberman, Alexander, 39–41, 44
Lindner, Richard, 74
Links, 14-karat, 47
Lord of the Flies (Golding), 157
Love Story, (Siegel), 78

McBride, Patricia, 52
McCarthy, Joe, 116
McNiel, Legs, 119
Madame of Madness (punk rock singer), 113
Makos, Christopher, vii, 129–143, 191
Malle, Louis, 53
Malpractice (punk rock album), 113
Malta, Silvano, 45
Manchurian Candidate (Condon), 167

Index

Index